Bags of Inspiration

15 elegant bags to make and embellish

Bags of Inspiration

15 elegant bags to make and embellish

Hilary Bowen

GUILD OF MASTER CRAFTSMAN PUBLICATIONS

First published 2006 by
Guild of Master Craftsman Publications Ltd
Castle Place, 166 High Street, Lewes, East Sussex, BN7 1XU

ISBN-13 978-186108-438-5

ISBN-10 1-86108-438-2

Production Manager: Hilary MacCallum
Managing Editor: Gerrie Purcell
Project Editor: Dominique Page
Managing Art Editor: Gilda Pacitti
Designer: Patricia Briggs

Set in Officina Sans
Colour origination by MRM Graphics.
Printed and bound in Singapore by Kyodo Printing Co.

Measurements Note: *Conversions are from metric and are approximate.*
Use either imperial or metric, do not mix units of measurement.

Contents

Project Preparation

Introduction

IMAGINE having bought (or perhaps even made) the perfect outfit for a wedding, party, or other occasion only to discover that you cannot find a bag to complement it, or searching for a gift but not being able to find quite what you're looking for. Well, now you can design your own bag that will make a unique gift and be appreciated by friends and family or provide an ideal accessory to your outfit for a fraction of the price that it would have cost you to buy.

The bags described and illustrated in this book are far more than merely functional items for holding a few essentials when you are out for the evening; their decorative appeal turns them into accessories almost akin to jewellery, which can enliven or add the perfect finishing touch to an ensemble. They can be made quickly and simply and on a limited budget. In fact, if you acquire your fabrics and trimmings from old or discarded clothes, they will cost you almost nothing.

These bags are exciting and fun to make. You will be using small quantities of beautiful fabrics, such as silks, satins, chiffons and velvets (or equally attractive synthetic versions), combined with gorgeous, glitzy metallic threads, which will provide the extra 'wow' factor. Add to that the other possible decorative embellishments, such as sequins, ribbons and beads, which will provide further sparkle, and your evening bags will be second to none. There is scope here for highly creative designs, which can be as minimalist or as 'over-the-top' as you wish.

However, this book is about more than making bags. Contained within these pages is a wide range of exciting techniques, which can be used to create texture and colour with fabric – techniques which can be applied to a much wider range of projects. These include (among others) embossing, ruching, slashing, quilting, pleating, cut-work and hand-dyeing.

I hope, therefore, that this book will be a valuable resource not only for people interested in designing and making bags, but also for those who enjoy manipulating and embellishing fabrics for other projects as well. Have fun!

Note: *The designs included vary in terms of complexity – some are very simple and can be made in a day, others require a bit more time, but all can be made by anyone who has basic sewing skills and a sewing machine.*

The Projects

Summer Foliage

A Bag with Appliquéd Leaf Motifs

This bag is one of a series of three incorporating leaf designs, each representing different seasons according to the colour theme. The one shown here represents summer, since the colours are beautiful shades of green. ('Autumn' and 'Winter' are shown on page 17.)

Materials

- One piece of scrunched viscose measuring 21 × 13 in (53 × 33 cm)
- One piece of fusible interfacing the same size and shape
- One piece of wadding measuring 21 × 6¼ in (53 × 16 cm)
- One piece of cord measuring 48 in (122 cm) for the handle
- A variety of small pieces of decorative fabrics for the leaves (e.g. chiffon, silk, organza)
- A press-stud fastener
- Machine cotton
- Metallic threads for the motifs and the satin-stitching
- Optional: A selection of beads and small pieces of ribbon for the decoration in the corner of the bag

The background fabric used for the main body of the bag was scrunched viscose, hand-dyed to a rich green colour. The leaf motifs were given a glittery effect by the use of Angelina fibres sandwiched between layers of chiffon.

See **Creating Motifs**, pages 143–147

Instructions

Preparing the fabric

1 Make a number of leaf motifs, as described on pages 143–147. The number you make is up to you, but in this example six were used.

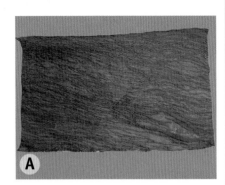

2 Take your piece of fabric for the main body of the bag **A**. Pin on the piece of fusible interfacing to the wrong side of the fabric and iron it in place **B**. Peel off the backing paper.

3 Place the piece of wadding over one half of the fabric onto the adhesive side. Iron it on until it has bonded with the adhesive **C**.

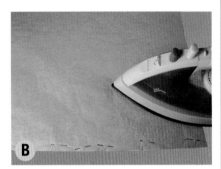

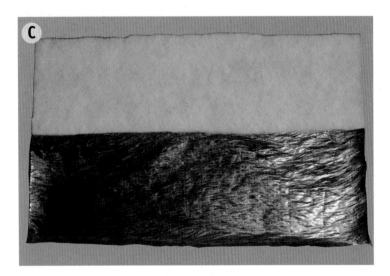

Note: *Either iron onto the non-adhesive side of the fabric or place a sheet of baking parchment (or similar) on top of the wadding before you iron; otherwise the wadding, and possibly some of the adhesive, will melt onto the bottom of your iron.*

Construction

4 With right sides together, fold the fabric in half lengthways and sew along two sides of the rectangle, leaving one short side and the 'fold' side unstitched.

5 Turn the bag right sides out **D**, then turn the bottom third up and pin and tack in place **E**.

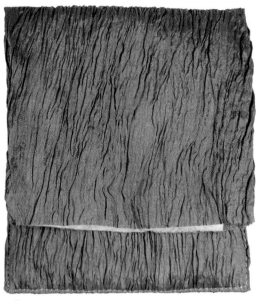

F   **G**

6 Now machine-stitch the sides to secure them in place (using ordinary machine cotton).

7 Using metallic thread in the sewing machine, satin-stitch all around the sides and bottom of the bag (do not stitch the flap). This will create a nice decorative edge and provide a professional-looking finish **F**.

8 Fold the top flap down over the main body of the bag **G**.

9 Next, take your leaf motifs and place each one right side up onto a piece of fusible interfacing **H**. Place a piece of paper over the top to protect your iron and iron the leaf to the interfacing so that the two are bonded **I**. Peel off the backing paper.

H

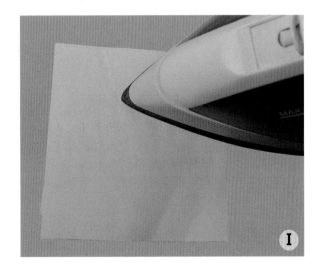

I

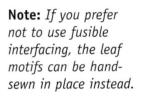

10 Cut away part of the bag flap at an angle and begin to place your leaf motifs in the desired positions J . Exactly how you decide to arrange them and how many you use is, of course, a matter of choice, but it is worth spending some time at this stage experimenting with different arrangements.

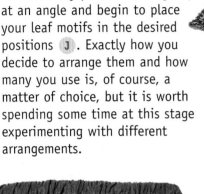

J

11 When you have decided on the position of the motifs, iron them in place so that they are fused to the bag flap. Notice how the leaves here have been placed so that they overhang and conceal the edge of the flap, creating a natural, random edge K .

Note: *If you prefer not to use fusible interfacing, the leaf motifs can be hand-sewn in place instead.*

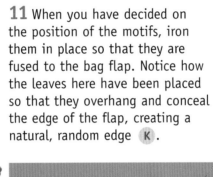

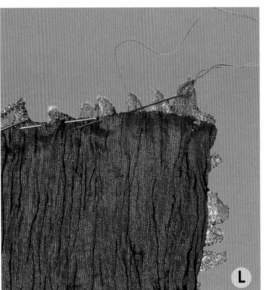

L

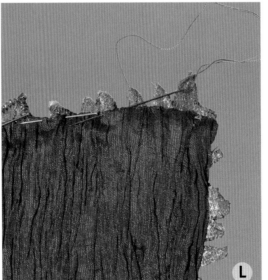

M

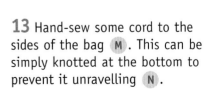

12 Now turn under the edges of the flap (on the underside), pin and hand-sew neatly so that there are no raw edges L .

13 Hand-sew some cord to the sides of the bag M . This can be simply knotted at the bottom to prevent it unravelling N .

N

14 Now attach a press-stud fastener, or similar (see page 107 for information on alternatives) to the underside of the bag flap.

15 Optional: A cluster of assorted beads and ribbon may be sewn in the bottom left-hand corner for further embellishment O. Alternatively, you could add a decorative trim of gathered ribbon to the bottom edge of the bag, as shown in photo Q.

O

Variations

As already mentioned, 'Summer' is one of three in a series of leaf bags. Photo P shows the 'Autumn' version, where a colour theme of reds and russets was used. Photo Q shows the 'Winter' version with pale blue and silver to represent a frosting of ice. Note that in this example, a different-shaped leaf has been used for the motif – ivy leaves. In all three examples the same techniques were used.

P

Q

Tutti Frutti

A Bag with Appliquéd Fruit Motifs

This is a delightful bag to make, and any type of fruit can be chosen for the decorative motifs. In this example the motifs are one slice of lemon, one slice of orange, two slices of kiwi fruit, one slice of water melon, one plum, two cherries and three blueberries. In addition, three 'blackberry' beads have been added.

Materials

- One piece of red satin measuring 23 × 16 in (58 × 40 cm)
- One piece of fusible interfacing measuring 23 × 8 in (58 × 20 cm)
- One piece of wadding measuring 23 × 8 in (58 × 20 cm)

- One length of cord measuring 48 in (122 cm)
- Machine thread
- A selection of scraps of decorative fabrics, such as chiffon, silk and organza for the motifs
- Metallic machine threads for the motifs

- One press-stud fastener
- Optional: Fusible interfacing to attach the motifs
- Optional: Three 'blackberry' beads for additional decoration
- Optional: Angelina fibres for the motifs

In this example, the blueberry motifs were made from circles of purple silk stuffed with cotton wool, creating a three-dimensional effect that contrasts with the other flat motifs.

See **Creating Motifs**, pages 141–142

Instructions

Preparing the fabric

1 Begin by making a variety of different fruit motifs following the instructions on pages 141–142.

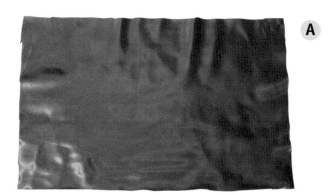

2 Cut out your piece of red satin to the dimensions given, or your prefer red dimensions **A**.

3 Iron on the fusible interfacing to one half of the wrong side of the fabric **B**.

4 Place the wadding on top of the area of adhesive left by the fusible interfacing, turn the fabric over and iron it from the other side of the fabric. Your wadding should now be bonded in place **C**.

Note: *Do not iron directly onto the wadding or it will melt and stick to the underside of your iron.*

Construction

5 With right sides together, fold the fabric in half lengthways and pin along two sides, leaving the 'fold' side and one short side unpinned 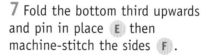.

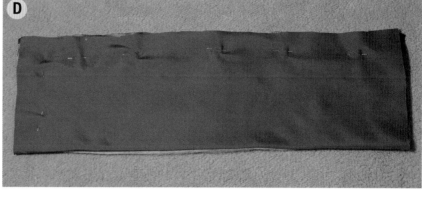

6 Tack and machine-stitch along the pinned sides then turn the fabric the right way out so that right sides are facing outwards and the wadding is on the inside.

7 Fold the bottom third upwards and pin in place then machine-stitch the sides 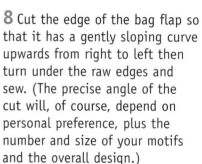.

8 Cut the edge of the bag flap so that it has a gently sloping curve upwards from right to left then turn under the raw edges and sew. (The precise angle of the cut will, of course, depend on personal preference, plus the number and size of your motifs and the overall design.)

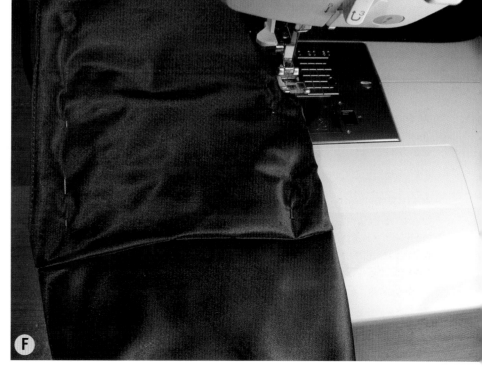

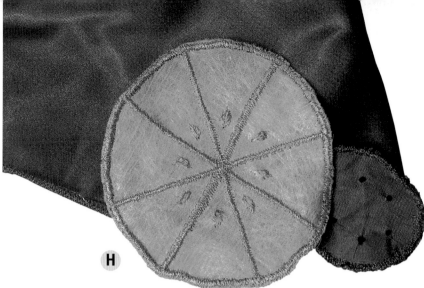

9 Using satin-stitch, sew around all the edges, including the bottom, sides and around the bag flap to give a decorative edge **G**.

10 Open out the bag flap and begin to arrange the motifs **H**. You may wish to spend some time trying different positions for the motifs until you find the most pleasing arrangement.

11 Iron on some fusible interfacing to the backs of your motifs and then iron them in position. (If you prefer, they can be hand-sewn in place.) Note the 'blackberry' beads, which have been sewn on for extra decoration **I**. Photo **J** shows the underside of the bag flap – note how the motifs overhang (and conceal) the edge.

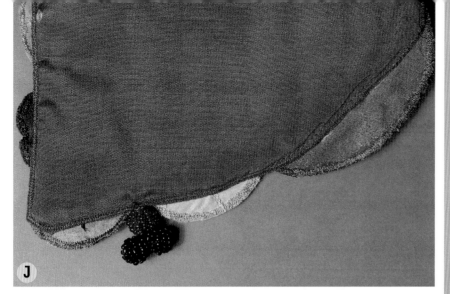

J

Variation

Photo  L shows another bag with fruit made in the same way; however, this time strawberries were made from red silk and stuffed with wadding before being sewn on to the bag flap.

12 Take the length of cord and pin it to the sides of the bag, then hand-sew it in place K.

13 Finally, attach a press-stud fastener to the underside of the bag flap.

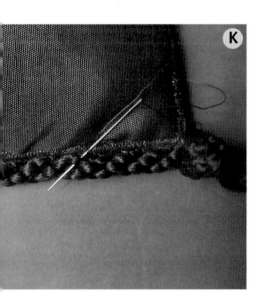

K

L

Fuchsias

A Bag with Appliquéd Flower Motifs

In spring and summer it is a delight to celebrate the fine weather and colourful flowers by wearing something which reflects this floral abundance. There are so many flowers to choose from, one really is spoilt for choice. However, the inspiration for this particular design was the beautiful shapes and colours of fuchsias.

Materials

- One piece of red satin measuring 21×13 in (53×33 cm)
- One piece of fusible interfacing measuring $21 \times 6\frac{1}{4}$ in (53×16 cm)
- One piece of wadding measuring $21 \times 6\frac{1}{4}$ in (53×16 cm)
- One piece of cord measuring 48 in (122 cm) for the handle
- Small pieces of green, pink and purple satin for the flowers
- Coloured wire and small beads for the flower stamens
- A press-stud fastener
- Machine cotton
- Red and green metallic threads

Here the fuchsia motifs were partly flat and partly three-dimensional – the lower petals are made from rolled sections of fabric which billow outwards. The stamens made from coloured wire and glass beads add extra interest.

See **Creating Motifs**, pages 150–151

Instructions

Preparing the fabric

1 Make a number of flower motifs according to your chosen design. Here, fuchsias have been used (see instructions for motifs on pages 150–151). The number you choose to create is up to you, but in this example three were used.

A

2 Take your piece of fabric for the main body of the bag (in this example red satin). Using fusible interfacing, bond the wadding to one half of the fabric on the wrong side 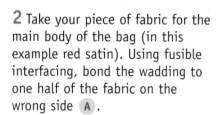 A .

Construction

3 With right sides together, fold the fabric in half lengthways and sew along two sides of the rectangle, leaving one short side and the 'fold' side unstitched.

B

4 Turn the bag right sides out B then turn the bottom third up and pin and tack it in place C .

5 Machine-stitch the sides to secure them using ordinary machine cotton. Then, using metallic thread in the sewing machine, satin-stitch all around the sides and bottom of the bag (but not the flap) D .

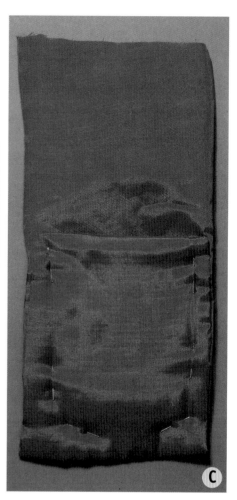

C

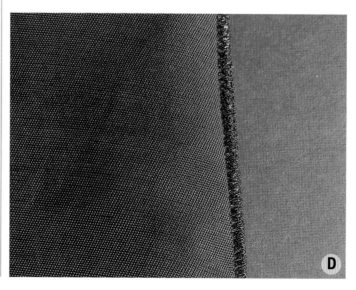

D

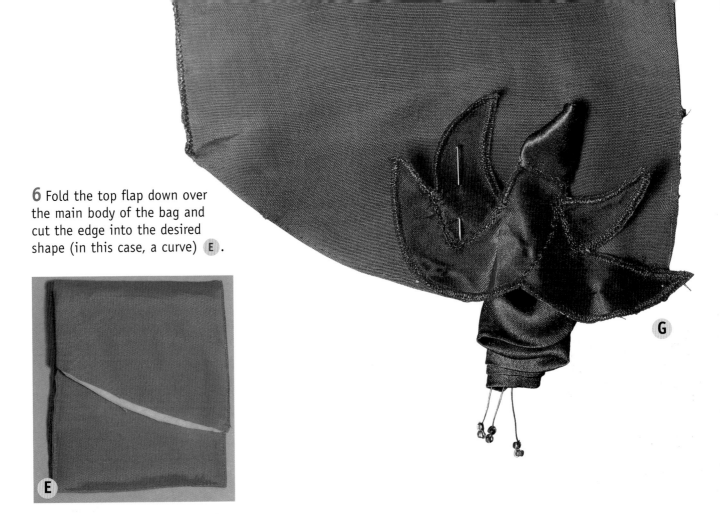

6 Fold the top flap down over the main body of the bag and cut the edge into the desired shape (in this case, a curve) **E**.

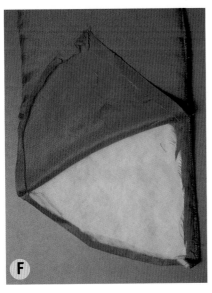

7 The flower motifs need to be sewn on the top face of the bag flap. However, you do not want visible stitching on the underside, as this would be unsightly. So, to avoid this, unpick the side of the flap to free the top face from the underside **F**. The underside can be re-attached later, after the motifs have been sewn in place.

8 Now begin to place the flower motifs in the desired positions. Exactly how you decide to arrange them and how many you use is a matter of choice, and it is worth spending some time at this stage experimenting with different arrangements. Here the flowers have been placed so that they overhang and conceal the edge of the flap, creating a natural random edge **G**.

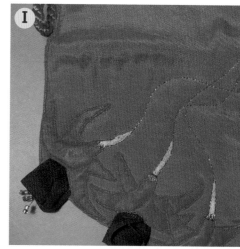

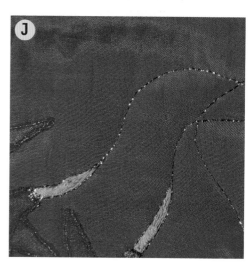

9 Once you have decided on the positions of the motifs, you need to secure them in place. For this bag, the petals of the fuchsias contained fusible interfacing adhesive on their undersides so that they could be ironed onto the bag fabric. However, the roll of purple petals had not been treated with adhesive, so the motifs also needed to be sewn as well as ironed in place **H**. Notice also that the flowers have been sewn directly onto the top face of the bag flap; however, if you wish to create a slightly 'quilted' effect you could place under this top face another layer of satin with a layer of wadding in between, to give the surface more 'depth'.

10 The stems of the flowers have been created by a mixture of decorative hand-stitching and machine-stitching with green metallic thread **I**. Photo **J** shows this in close-up.

11 Once all the sewing on the top face of the bag flap is complete, bring up the underneath side and hand-stitch it neatly in place **K**.

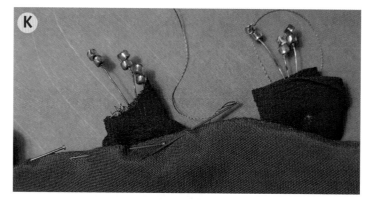

12 Next, hand-sew some cord to the sides of the bag **L**. This can be simply knotted at the bottom to prevent it unravelling.

13 Finally, attach a press-stud fastener (or similar) to the underside of the bag flap.

Variations

Photo ⓜ shows a bag with very different flower embellishments. The flowers have been made from gold ribbon with gathered wire along one edge. The centres of each have been decorated with gold beads. The remainder of the bag has been further embellished with feathers and gold trim, with gold furnishing tassels sewn along the bottom edge. Photo ⓝ shows the flowers in close-up.

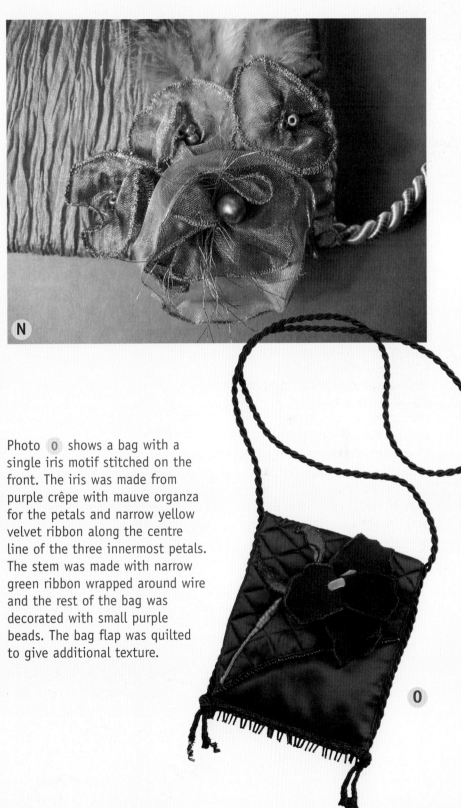

Photo ⓞ shows a bag with a single iris motif stitched on the front. The iris was made from purple crêpe with mauve organza for the petals and narrow yellow velvet ribbon along the centre line of the three innermost petals. The stem was made with narrow green ribbon wrapped around wire and the rest of the bag was decorated with small purple beads. The bag flap was quilted to give additional texture.

Butterfly

A Bag with Appliquéd Butterfly Motif

The inspiration for this design came from the beautiful colours and shapes of butterflies, of which there are so many. I used a length of mauve satin for the main fabric and then for the butterfly motif, a variety of small pieces of fabric, including chiffon, satin, organza, plus Angelina fibres, silver gutta, coloured wire and small beads.

Materials

- One piece of mauve satin measuring 21 × 13 in (53 × 33 cm)
- One piece of fusible interfacing measuring 21 × 6¼ in (53 × 16 cm)
- One piece of wadding measuring 21 × 6¼ in (53 × 16 cm)

- One piece of mauve cord measuring 48 in (122 cm) for the handle
- Small pieces of mauve satin, chiffon and organza for the butterfly
- Coloured wire and small beads for the antennae
- A small piece of cotton wool for the body of the butterfly

- Angelina fibres
- A press-stud fastener
- Machine cotton
- Different shades of mauve metallic threads
- Optional: Lace trim and small beads

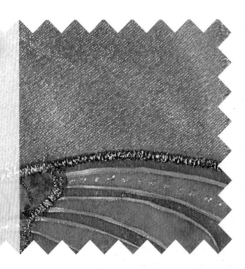

The butterfly motif is the most challenging of all the motifs in this book, as it requires the assembly of five sections. The 'body' of the insect is a hollow tube of organza stuffed with cotton wool.

See **Creating Motifs**, pages 152–155

Instructions

Preparing the fabric

1 Make the butterfly motif according to the instructions on pages 152–155 or, alternatively, make up your own design.

2 Using fusible interfacing, bond the wadding to one half of your main fabric on the wrong side .

A

Construction

3 With right sides together, fold the fabric in half lengthways and sew along two sides of the rectangle, leaving one short side and the 'fold' side unstitched.

4 Turn the bag right sides out **B** then turn the bottom third up and pin and tack in place **C**.

B

C

D

5 Machine-stitch the sides to secure them in place, using ordinary machine cotton. Then, using metallic thread in the sewing machine, satin-stitch all around the sides and bottom of the bag (but not the flap) **D**.

E

F

6 Position the butterfly motif so that nearly all of it is covering the bag flap but allow the edges to overhang E. The edges of the bag flap will need to be trimmed so that they do not show.

7 When you have decided on the exact position for the butterfly, fix it onto the bag flap: either use fusible interfacing and heat-bond it in place with an iron, or hand-stitch it in place. In fact, I would recommend doing both, so that it is really secure.

8 After trimming the bottom of the bag flap so that it follows the contours of the motif, turn under the raw edges and neatly hand-sew them.

9 Now hand-sew some mauve cord along the sides of the bag F. This can be simply knotted at the bottom to prevent it unravelling.

10 Attach a press-stud fastener (or similar) to the underside of the bag flap.

11 Optional: For additional decoration, some lace trim embellished with small beads may be attached to the bottom of the bag G.

G

Winter Days

A Bag made from Shirred Velvet

During the depths of winter I was inspired to make a bag that would be warm, rich and tactile to use. I found a length of beautiful burgundy velvet and decided that by using a shirring technique I could add further texture. I sewed a rosette on to the side for a final decoration.

Materials

- A piece of shirred velvet of sufficient dimensions to make the bag of your chosen size. In this example, the dimensions were $23 \times 8\frac{1}{4}$in $(58 \times 21$cm$)$. The original piece of unshirred velvet was 36×22in $(91 \times 55$cm$)$

- A piece of the same velvet material for the strap, measuring 45×2in $(115 \times 5$cm$)$
- Machine cotton
- Silk for the bag lining measuring $23 \times 8\frac{1}{4}$in $(58 \times 21$cm$)$
- A selection of beads

- Ribbon
- Fusible interfacing
- Some small scraps of the same velvet and silk to make the rosette. Each piece needs to be approximately 8×4in $(20 \times 10$cm$)$
- A press-stud fastener

When velvet is shirred it becomes quite thick. So instead of constructing the bag according to the instructions in Making the Basic Bag, where the fabric is folded in half lengthways to form the lining, I chose silk lining. Your shirred fabric does not have to be velvet, though. Variations could include satin, silk, or synthetic versions of either. If you choose silk, you could hand-dye it first, in a variety of different shades, to give a pleasing effect when shirred.

See **Special Effects, Shirring**, pages 116–119

Instructions

Preparing the fabric

1 Prepare your piece of double-shirred velvet according to the instructions on pages 116–119 . When finished it should measure about $23 \times 8\frac{1}{4}$in (58×21cm).

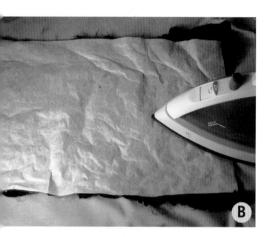

2 Place your shirred velvet face down and iron onto the back a piece of fusible interfacing that has been cut to the same size **B**. This will ensure the shirred velvet does not become distorted.

3 Peel off the backing paper **C** then with right sides together, pin the shirred velvet to the silk **D**.

Construction

4 Sew the shirred velvet and silk together all the way around except for one short edge. Fold the right sides out. You should now have a rectangle with shirred velvet on one side and the lining silk on the other.

5 With the silk side uppermost, fold up the bottom third to the required height and mark with pins or thread (along the fold) the height to which it has been folded up. In this example the height was 7 in (18 cm).

6 Turn the bag section inside out, so the velvet side is uppermost, and pin the bottom third up to the same height as before.

7 Stitch a curve on each corner to round them off and trim away the excess fabric **E**. Turn right sides out again. The bottom corners will now be curved.

8 Repeat this on the edges of the bag flap, by cutting off the corners into a similar shape.

9 To finish the edge of the bag flap fold over to the inside about 3/8 in (1 cm) of the raw edge of the shirred velvet and pin in place. Bring up the edge of the silk lining, turning over the raw edge to the inside as you go. Pin and hand-sew in place to finish off the edge neatly **F**.

10 Make the shoulder strap by cutting a piece of the unshirred velvet to 45 × 2in (115 × 5cm). With right sides together, fold in half lengthways and pin. Cut the ends into short points.

11 To make the strap firmer, iron on a length of interfacing along one side.

12 Sew the raw edges together leaving a gap at one end G.

13 Turn this inside out through the gap, so that the right sides are on the outside. Hand-sew the edges to close the gap and press flat.

14 Using the sewing machine, neatly top-stitch along each edge of the strap, to give a professional finish.

15 Pin the shoulder strap in place at either side of the bag so that the points meet the tops of the stitched curve towards the lower end of the bag sides. With wrong sides together, top-stitch the sides of the strap to the sides of the bag. The shoulder strap now effectively forms a side gusset to give the bag greater depth H.

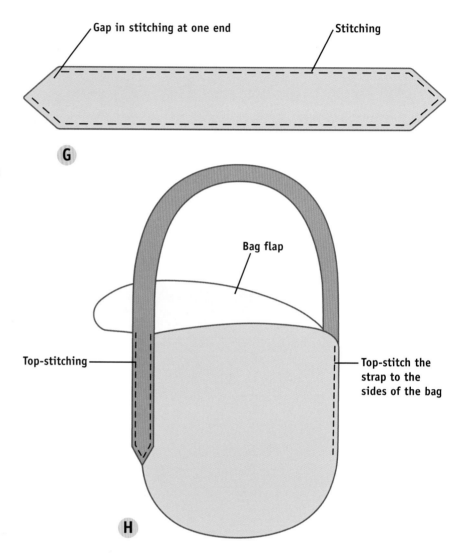

Gap in stitching at one end

Stitching

G

Bag flap

Top-stitching

Top-stitch the strap to the sides of the bag

H

16 Optional: Make a rosette by cutting two identical circles of unshirred velvet 5in (13 cm) in diameter. With right sides together, sew all around the edge leaving a small gap of about 1in (3cm). Turn inside out through the gap, so that the velvet sides are uppermost. Hand-stitch the gap closed.

17 Cut a small hole about 1in (3cm) in diameter through the middle of both circles. Hand-stitch a large running stitch all around this hole, approximately ¼in (0.5 cm) from the hole edge I. (Note: In the photo, white thread was used to illustrate the step more clearly but in practice you would use thread of the same colour as your fabric.)

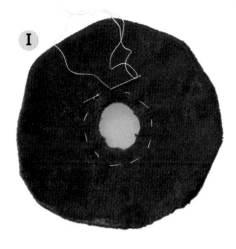

I

18 Pull the thread taut so that the fabric is gathered up in the centre. Fasten off the thread J.

19 Make another rosette slightly smaller than the first, using the same silk fabric as the lining. The dimensions of the first circles should be about 4 in (10 cm).

20 Sew the two rosettes together and embellish with a decorative bead and some ribbon. Photo K shows the finished rosette.

21 Hand-sew the rosette on to the top corner of the bag flap.

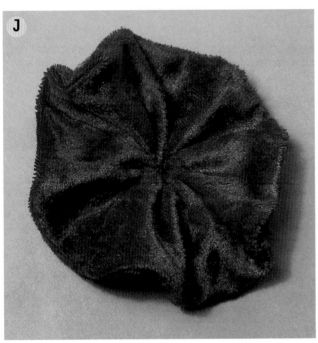

J

K

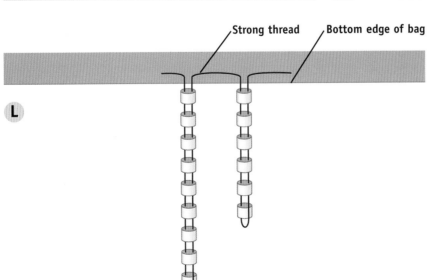

L

Strong thread   Bottom edge of bag

22 Optional: As a final decoration you can sew some beads to the bottom edge of the bag. For this bag, long strings of graduated lengths were sewn all along the bottom edge L.

23 Finally, attach a press-stud to your bag.

Shimmering Mist

A Bag made from Ruched Organza

For this bag I wanted to create a light and airy effect, but at the same time obtain a feeling of 'richness'. Organza, with its wonderful shimmery sheen, seemed ideal for this project. The addition of tiny seed beads adds extra sparkle.

Materials

- Organza:
  23^1/$_2$ × 15 in (60 × 38 cm) for the basic bag
  47 × 16 in (120 × 40 cm) for the ruching layer
  40 × 7 in (102 × 18 cm) for the handle
  40 × 1^1/$_2$ in (102 × 4 cm) for the gathered trim
- Wadding measuring 24 × 7^1/$_2$ in (60 × 19 cm)
- Strong thread for hand-sewing
- Machine thread
- A press-stud fastener
- Optional: Seed beads

For this bag, the ruching technique is used. This effect extends across the back and flap of the bag, while the front has been left plain.

See **Special Effects, Ruching**, pages 120–122

Instructions

Preparing the fabric

1 Take the piece of 23½ × 15 in (60 × 38 cm) organza and sew the wadding along one half of it **A**.

2 Turn the fabric and wadding over so that the organza is uppermost. Mark off a section measuring 16 in (40 cm) in length and half the width of the fabric, i.e. 7½ in (19 cm) **B**. This is the area that will bear the ruched fabric and is also the area that will form the back and flap of the bag.

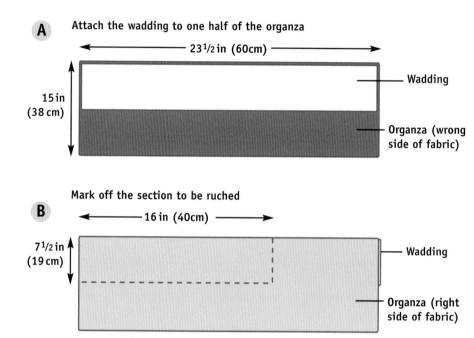

A Attach the wadding to one half of the organza

23½ in (60cm)

15 in (38 cm)

Wadding

Organza (wrong side of fabric)

B Mark off the section to be ruched

16 in (40cm)

7½ in (19 cm)

Wadding

Organza (right side of fabric)

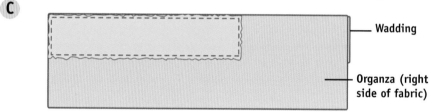

C Layer of organza, gathered on all four sides and stitched to base layer

Wadding

Organza (right side of fabric)

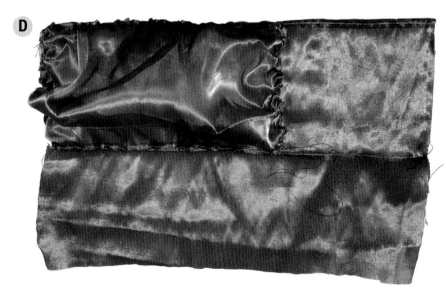

D

3 Take the piece of 47 × 16 in (120 × 40 cm) organza and sew a running stitch around the edge on all four sides. Place this on top of the section of organza marked out to receive the ruching layer, i.e. the section measuring 16 × 7½ in (40 × 19 cm). Tack the gathered layer onto the flat organza so the edges lie along the 16 × 7½ in (40 × 19cm) boundary. Machine-stitch this in place and remove the tacking stitches and the running stitch **C D**.

4 Now carry out the ruching method as described on pages 120–122. Photo **E** shows the partially ruched section. Continue with the ruching until you reach a stage where you consider it to be finished.

5 Optional: Sew seed beads in clusters in the 'troughs' of the ruching **F**. Now that the ruched section of the fabric is finished, the bag may be sewn up as described overleaf.

Construction

6 With right sides together fold the fabric in half lengthways and stitch along one short side and the long side opposite the fold – refer to step 3 on page 110 then continue with steps 4–6 (pages 110–111) to make up the basic bag shape. Photo G shows the bottom third of the bag folded and pinned in place.

G

H

7 Finish the edge of the bag flap by turning under the raw edge on the underside then pinning and hand-sewing in place H. Now make the handle as described in steps 8–9.

8 Take the length of organza measuring 40 × 7in (102 × 18cm) and cut it into three strips lengthways. On each one, fold under all the raw edges and top-stitch.

9 Secure the three lengths together at one end and plait them along the whole length **I**. With thread, neatly fasten off both ends of the plait and hand-sew it in place along the sides of the bag.

I

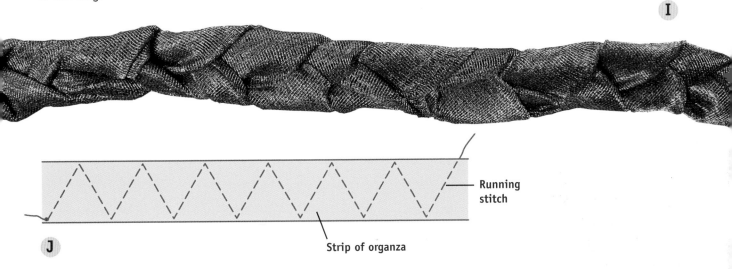

Running stitch

J

Strip of organza

10 Optional: Make a length of trim to sew along the bottom of the bag. Take the 40 × 1½ in (102 × 4cm) piece of organza and fold it in half lengthways. Machine-stitch it along the long open side and one of the short sides. Turn this inside out and press flat with a cool iron. Using strong thread the same colour as the organza, sew a running stitch along its length in a zigzag fashion **J**. Pull the thread taut and the fabric will be drawn up and gathered **K**. Secure the running thread so that this trim is the required length and sew it along the bottom edge of the bag.

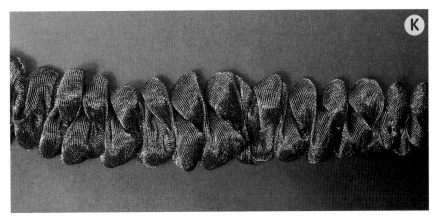

K

11 Finally, attach your press-stud fastener.

Checkerboard

A Bag made from Woven Ribbon

This is a bold, eye-catching design. It is in the 'clutch' style, so it doesn't have a handle or a strap, but you can attach either of these if you wish. The square shapes created by the woven ribbon reflect the geometric, rectangular design of the bag, which was inspired by the game of checkers.

Materials

- A piece of ribbon-weave fabric measuring approximately 20½ × 12½ in (52 × 32 cm). Four different colours of ribbon were used, each ⅝ in (1.5 cm) in width. Lengths of 236 in (600 cm) for each colour were needed to make a piece of fabric this size
- Machine cottons, including optional metallic thread
- Wadding measuring 20½ × 6¼ in (52 × 16 cm)
- Fusible interfacing measuring 20½ × 7½ in (52 × 16 cm)
- One press-stud fastener
- One decorative glass bead or button
- About 40 in (100cm) of ⅝ in (1.5 cm) ribbon for edging

To economize on ribbon, you could make a piece of ribbon-weave fabric that is only half the specified width, i.e. 20½ × 6¼ in (52 × 16 cm). This could then be sewn to a piece of silk of the same size, and the two pieces then sewn together. The silk will become, in effect, the lining.

See **Special Effects, Ribbon Weaving**, pages 123–124

Instructions

Preparing the fabric

1 Prepare your piece of ribbon-weave fabric according to the instructions on pages 123–124.

2 Cut out the fabric and wadding, following the dimensions stated in the materials list. Fold the fabric right sides together lengthways then pin and tack the wadding to it so that all sides and corners match up.

Construction

3 Now make up the basic bag following steps 3–5 (see pages 110–111) A.

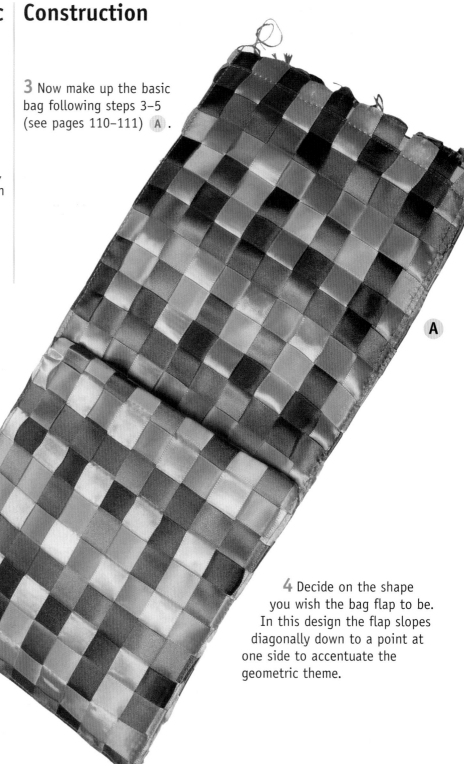

A

4 Decide on the shape you wish the bag flap to be. In this design the flap slopes diagonally down to a point at one side to accentuate the geometric theme.

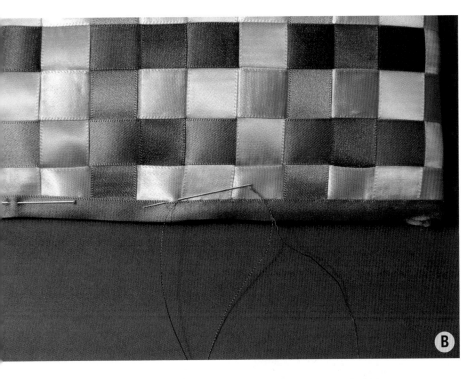

6 Sew a length of ribbon all around the edge of the bag to provide a neat finish ⓑ.

7 Lastly, attach a press-stud fastening on the underside of the flap corner and sew a decorative glass bead or button on top ⓒ.

5 Turn the raw edges of the bag flap in towards each other at a depth of approximately ⅝ in (1.5cm), then neatly pin and hand-sew the edges together.

Note: *It is important not to distort the shape while sewing, so you may wish to tack the edges together after pinning and before the final sewing.*

Evening Light

A Bag with a Mexican Pleat Design

This bag is ideal for a special evening out. The choice of colour and two-tone fabric was inspired by the beautiful changing colours of evening light as dusk descends. The key word here is 'texture'. Mexican pleats create a three-dimensional effect that is very attractive. The two-tone fabric suits the pleats too; because they sit at very slight angles to each other, the light hits them from different directions

Materials

- A piece of fabric measuring 24 × 9in (60 × 22cm) for the panel of Mexican pleats
- A piece of the same fabric measuring 24 × 13½in (60 × 34cm) for the main body of the bag

- A piece of the same fabric measuring approximately 33 × 3in (84 × 7cm) for the handle. (You may wish to make the handle longer or shorter than this.)
- Machine cottons

- Wadding measuring 24 × 7in (60 × 17cm)
- Fusible interfacing measuring 24 × 7in (60 × 17cm)
- A press-stud fastener or magnetic fastener
- A temporary marking pen

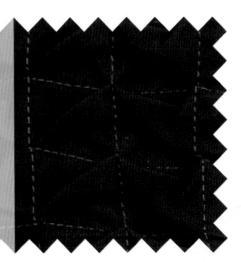

Mexican Pleats are easier to construct if your material is stretchy; even better if elasticated. This bag is constructed from slighly elasticated nylon. Note too that the dimensions are different to those described in Making the Basic Bag to accommodate the final size of the pleated fabric.

See **Special Effects**, **Mexican Pleats**, pages 128–130

Instructions

Preparing the fabric

1 Take your piece of 24 × 9in (60 × 22cm) fabric and draw horizontal parallel lines on it with a temporary marking pen. The lines need to go from one long side to the other and alternate between 1³/₁₆in and ²/₃in (3 and 2 cm) apart 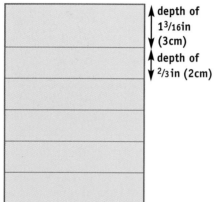.

2 Take the pairs of lines that are 1³/₁₆in (3 cm) apart and pin pairs together along their length. You should now have 12 pinned pleats **B**.

depth of 1³/₁₆in (3cm)

depth of ²/₃in (2cm)

A

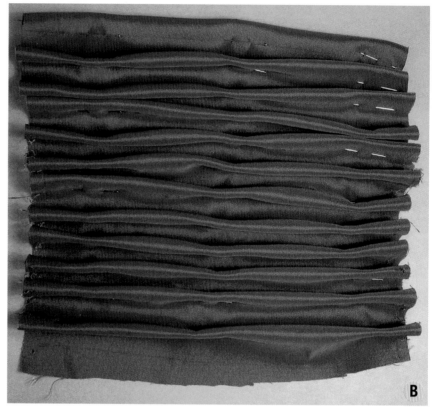

B

3 Tack along the lines, then remove the pins and machine-stitch along these lines **C**. Your fabric will now be much shorter – approximately 9¹/₂in (24 cm) – and the width may have reduced slightly.

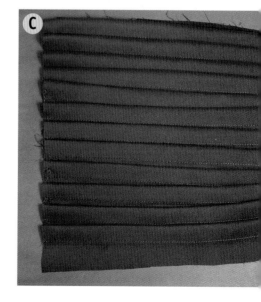

C

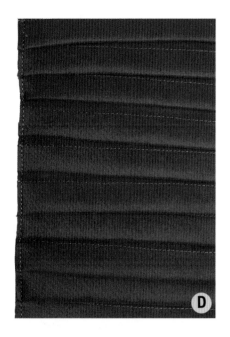

4 Machine-stitch a vertical line on top of the pleats along the left-hand edge of your piece of fabric D. This anchors the pleats in place.

5 Starting at the top, pin each pleat upwards approximately 1 in (2.5 cm) from the stitched anchor-line E. Now tack the pleats in place, remove the pins and machine-stitch.

6 Pin the pleats back down again about 1 in (2.5 cm) to the right of the previously stitched line F. Tack and machine-stitch as before.

7 Repeat the previous two steps until all the pleats have been stitched up and down, right across to the right-hand edge of the fabric.

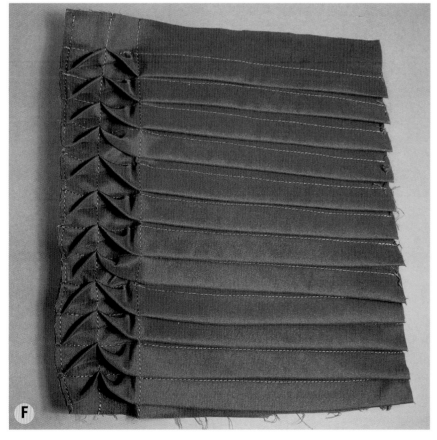

G

8 Now take the piece of fabric that measures 24 × 13½ in (60 × 34 cm) and, using fusible interfacing, iron on the piece of wadding to one half **G**. (If you prefer, you can sew the wadding in place instead of using fusible interfacing.)

9 The pleated section now needs to be attached to the part of the bag fabric that will become the flap, which is one sixth of the total area at this stage. Take the pleated fabric and turn under two of the edges. Pin these edges onto the appropriate section of the bag fabric, leaving the other two overhanging the edge of the bag fabric by approximately ³/₈ in (1 cm) **H** **I**. Tack, remove the pins and then machine top-stitch these two edges in place. (The overhanging raw edges will disappear when you make up the bag in the next step.)

Construction

10 With right sides together, fold the bag fabric in half lengthways and stitch along two edges in the normal way for constructing the basic bag (see steps 3–4 on pages 110–111), then turn inside out.

11 To make the handle, take your piece of fabric measuring 33 × 3 in (84 × 7 cm) and iron on some fusible interfacing **J**.

H

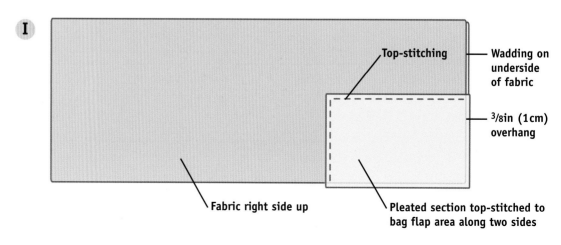

I

Top-stitching — Wadding on underside of fabric

— ³/₈in (1cm) overhang

Fabric right side up

Pleated section top-stitched to bag flap area along two sides

12 With right sides together, fold the fabric in half lengthways and sew along one long side and one short side **K**. Turn inside out and press. Fold in the raw edges of the unstitched short end and hand-sew together. Your handle can now be attached to the bag.

13 Fold the bottom third of your bag fabric rectangle upwards. Pin one end of the handle strap in place to both sides of the bottom half of the bag **L**.

14 Tack, remove the pins and machine top-stitch the handles in place **M**.

15 Turn the raw edges of the bag flap in towards each other at a depth of about ⅝ in (1.5 cm), then carefully pin and hand-sew the edges together neatly **N**.

16 Lastly, decide what type of fastening you would like. In this example a press-stud fastening has been used and the two halves of the press-stud were sown in their respective positions under the bag flap.

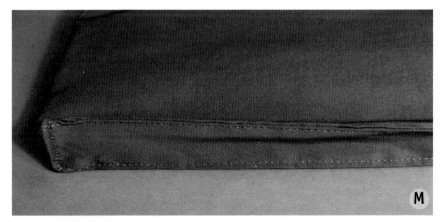

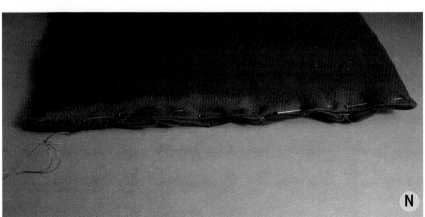

Golden Leaf

A Bag using the Cut-work Technique

This bag has a regal feel to it due to the use of purple and gold, which are royal colours. Once again, a theme from nature is evident, as a leaf shape was the starting point for the design. However, any motif could be used, provided it is fairly simplistic.

Materials

- A piece of purple satin measuring 23 × 16 in (58 × 40 cm) for the main body of the bag
- An additional piece of the same fabric measuring approximately 8 × 7½ in (20 × 19 cm) for the back of the bag flap

- Another piece of the same fabric measuring 51 × 4 in (130 × 10 cm) for the strap
- A piece of gold fabric measuring approximately 12 × 9 in (30 × 22 cm) – the size is not critical but it needs to be larger than the dimensions of your motif

- An additional piece of gold fabric for the strap, 51 × 4 in (130 × 10 cm)
- Fusible interfacing
- A piece of wadding measuring 23 × 8 in (58 × 20 cm)
- Machine thread
- A press-stud fastener

Shiny gold fabric was used here for the leaf motif, but any colour could be used, provided it contrasts with the surrounding fabric.

See **Special Effects, Cut-work**, pages 131–132

Instructions

Preparing the fabric

1 Take your piece of satin measuring 23 × 16 in (58 × 40 cm). Iron a piece of fusible interfacing measuring 8 × 7½ in (20 × 19 cm) to the wrong side of the fabric over the area that is to become the bag flap  **A**. This occupies one sixth of the total fabric and will be located in one corner **B**.

2 Now take the piece of satin measuring 8 × 7½ in (20 × 19 cm) and iron it onto the interfacing. This will strengthen the area onto which the motif will be transferred.

3 Select a design for your motif. In this example a leaf motif has been used **C**.

Wrong side of fabric

Fusible interfacing

Section of fabric ironed on top of interfacing

B

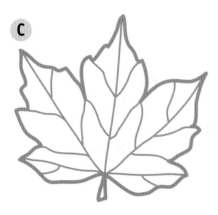

C

4 Transfer the design onto the right side of your fabric in the area that is to become the bag flap. A temporary fabric marker can be used for drawing the design onto the fabric. Using satin-stitch, machine-stitch along the drawn lines on the right side of the fabric **D**.

D

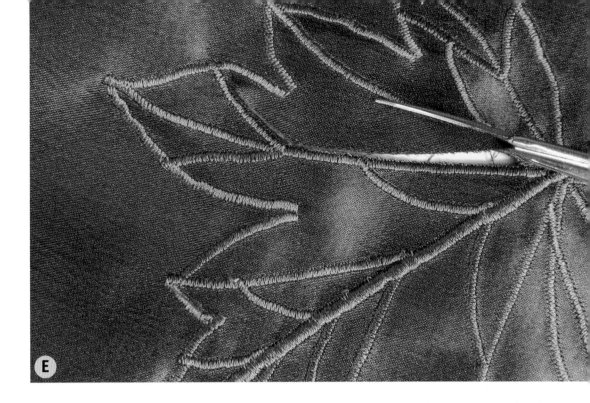

E

5 With small, sharp scissors, cut away the fabric from between the sewn lines. Snip as close as you can to the lines, but be careful not to cut through the thread **E**. (See also 'Tip' on page 61.)

6 Now take your piece of gold fabric and place it underneath the motif. Fix it in place with iron-on fusible interfacing or fabric adhesive.

7 Carefully top-stitch along the vein lines of the leaf. This helps to secure the motif to the gold fabric underneath and gives a nice finish **F**.

F

Construction

8 Now that the design on the bag flap is complete you are ready to make up the bag. Attach the wadding to the top half of the fabric on the wrong side, either by using fusible interfacing or by sewing. Make up the remainder of the bag following steps 2–5 on pages 109–111.

9 Cut the raw edge of the bag flap into a semi-circular shape. Turn the raw edges under towards each other, then pin and hand-sew the edges together.

10 To create an attractive finish along the edge of the bag flap, top-stitch in satin-stitch using gold thread all around the edge of the flap. Continue along the sides and the bottom edge of the bag **G**.

11 To make the strap, take the three pieces of fabric measuring 51 × 4 in (130 × 10 cm) – two in purple satin and one in gold fabric – and fold each one in half lengthways with right sides together. Sew along the raw edges to form a tube, then turn inside out.

12 Plait the pieces together to form the strap **H** then knot each end.

13 Align each end of the strap with the bottom edges of the bag and sew the strap to the sides of the bag **I**.

14 Lastly, attach the press-stud fastener.

Tip

When using scissors to cut away the fabric in between the sewn lines, it can sometimes be difficult to get close enough to the threads without cutting through them. There is also the possibility that the fabric may fray. There is a quicker, easier and neater way of cutting the fabric away from in between the sewn lines, which also prevents fraying. It involves using a soldering iron with a pointed tip. Place your fabric face up on a clean piece of glass. With a hot soldering iron, run the tip of the iron along the fabric where you wish to cut. The fabric will be cut quickly and neatly and the edges will be fused so that they cannot fray J . BUT, there are two very important factors that you need to take into account:

1 The fabric MUST be synthetic, otherwise it will not melt and fuse. Polyester and other synthetic fabrics are fine. You cannot use this technique on natural fabrics, such as cotton, wool, silk or linen.

2 You MUST use a type of thread which will not melt. Cotton and rayon threads are fine. Polyester thread is not suitable.

If you are in any doubt about which fabrics and threads are likely to melt, test them first with a hot soldering iron and see what happens. For further information on using a soldering iron to cut and fuse fabric, see Fusing Fabric by Margaret Beal. She also supplies the soldering irons (see 'Suppliers', on page 170).

Peacock Feathers

A Bag made from Hand-dyed Silk

This is a wonderful bag to make, and the silk painting effects can be really stunning. The dyes give vibrant colours to the silk, and the quilting enhances the lustre of the fabric. The inspiration for this bag was peacock feathers and this is reflected in the pattern and the bright, iridescent blues.

Materials

- A piece of silk measuring 25 × 16 in (64 × 40 cm)
- Some wadding of the same dimensions
- Backing material of the same dimensions
- A piece of mauve silk of the same dimensions for the lining
- Another piece of the same silk measuring 16 × 8½ in (40 × 22 cm) for the pocket

- A piece of dyed silk measuring 38 × 4 in (96 × 10 cm) for the shoulder strap
- A piece of wadding for the strap of the same dimensions
- A piece of fusible interfacing of the same dimensions for the strap
- Machine cotton

- Either a magnetic clasp or a decorative button and decorative elastic for the fastening
- A zip for the pocket, measuring approximately 7 in (18 cm)
- A selection of different-coloured dyes

This bag is similar to the Basic Bag design on pages 108–115, except that it is wider. Also, separate lining material has been used.

See **Special Effects, Silk Painting**, pages 136–139

Instructions

Preparing the fabric

1 First draw a design, such as this pattern of interlocking peacock feathers, onto paper .

2 Pin your silk onto a wooden frame, making sure it is taut 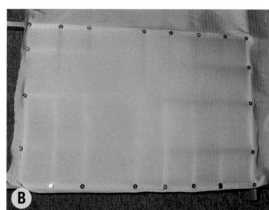.

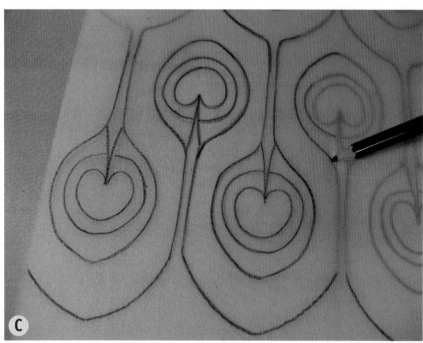

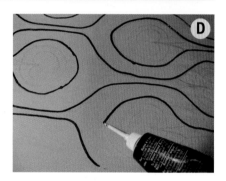

3 Place the frame so that the silk surface is in contact with the table top and slide your design underneath, aligned the way you want it. Then with a pencil, dark crayon or temporary marker, trace over the lines onto the silk C.

4 Now turn the frame over so that there is a gap between the silk and the table. Trace over the lines using black gutta D. Leave the gutta to dry thoroughly.

5 Having selected your dyes, paint carefully in between the gutta lines E. Do not overload your brush: even if the gutta lines are thick with no gaps, if the area of silk is too wet the dye will tend to 'bleed' through the gutta lines. Photo F shows a detail of the design after all the colours have been painted in.

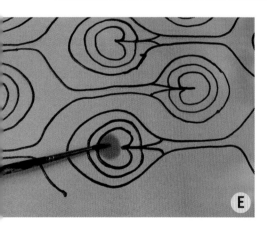

6 Optional: With gold gutta, paint thin gold lines to represent feather filaments 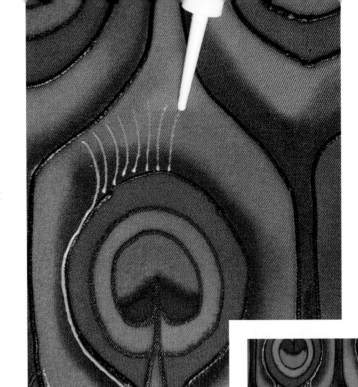 G. Leave to dry thoroughly. Photo H shows the design after the application of the gold gutta detail.

7 Now place the silk right side up on the wadding and place these two on top of the backing material to form a sandwich with the wadding in the middle. Pin them together, then tack and remove the pins.

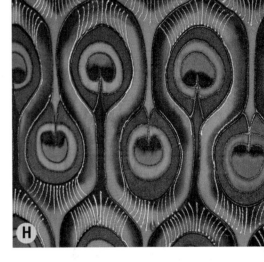

8 Machine-stitch along some of the gutta lines to create a lovely quilted effect. Don't try to do all of them, choose those you want to do and stick to those I. Remove the tacking stitches and you will now have a piece of beautifully dyed and quilted silk ready for making up into the bag.

Construction

9 Use the mauve silk lining to attach the zipped pocket. With right sides together, place the lining on top of the quilted fabric. Ensure that you align the lining so that the zipped pocket will be in the correct position when turned inside out. Pin and tack in place. Machine-stitch along three sides, leaving the edge that is to become the bottom of the bag flap unstitched. Turn inside out. You should now have your quilted silk with the mauve silk lining attached, and the pocket with the zip uppermost, as in photo **J**.

10 To prepare the shoulder strap, take your piece of silk measuring 38 × 4in (96 × 10cm) and iron on the fusible interfacing. Peel off the backing paper then iron on the wadding **K**. Now sew the side seams of the strap so that they taper towards the ends **L**.

11 Optional: Machine-stitch parallel lines along the length of the strap **M**.

12 Taking your quilted fabric with the lining uppermost, fold the bottom third up and pin in place. Mark the bottom of the fold, then sew the strap onto the sides of the bag, so that the pointed end of the strap meets the fold at the bottom of the bag **N**.

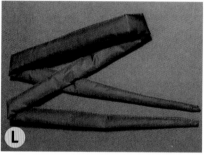

O

P

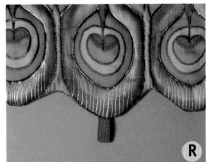

R

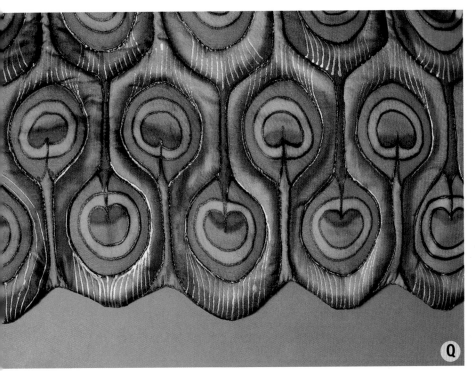

Q

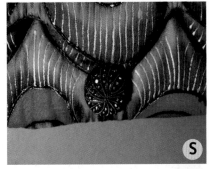

S

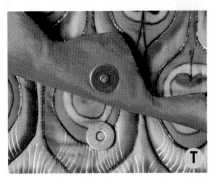

T

13 Optional: Sew additional motifs onto the shoulder strap for further decoration **O**.

14 Scallop the edge of the bag flap by cutting around the motifs, leaving an excess of fabric around each one of about 3/16 in (2cm). Then fold it under and pin it. Now do the same with the lining fabric and pin it in place **P**.

15 Hand-sew the lining to the rest of the fabric. Photo **Q** shows the finished scalloped edge.

16 For the fastening, either attach a decorative loop of elastic to the edge of the flap **R** and loop this around a decorative button **S** or attach a magnetic fastener **T**.

Animal

A Bag using the Embossing Technique

The starting point for this bag was a pair of fantastic acrylic handles which have a design suggesting animal prints. I wanted to echo the pattern in the handles by creating the impression of an animal print fabric in a warm, rich colour, which was also soft to touch.

Materials

- A piece of golden velvet measuring 24 × 16in (60 × 40cm)
- Backing fabric measuring 15 × 12in (38 × 30cm)
- Wadding of the same dimensions
- Lining material of the same dimensions
- Embroidery hoop
- A pair of acrylic handles with slots in the ends
- Fusible interfacing for the handle-band
- A press-stud or magnetic fastener
- Plenty of machine embroidery thread for the embossing (this technique uses a lot of thread)

I took some plain white velvet and hand-dyed it to a gorgeous golden colour, then used semi-metallic brown machine thread for all the sewing. The embossing effect adds to the tactile quality of the fabric, giving it soft texture and depth.

See **Special Effects, Embossing,** pages 125–127

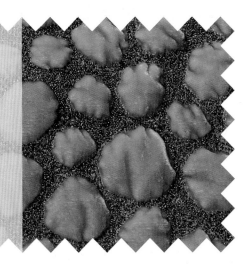

Instructions

Preparing the fabric

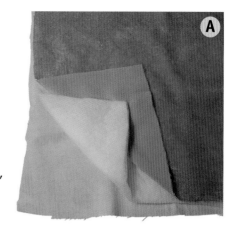

1 From your velvet cut a piece that measures 15 × 12in (38 × 30cm). This will form the main body of the bag. Put the remaining velvet to one side.

2 Now cut a piece of wadding and a piece of scrap material the same size as the cut velvet.

3 Pin all three pieces together with the wadding in the middle and the right side of the velvet facing outwards to form a 'sandwich' **A** .

4 With the scrap fabric uppermost, draw a random pattern of different-sized circles **B** . (If you prefer, this design can be drawn onto the scrap fabric before you pin the layers together.)

5 To your sewing machine, attach a 'free-style' embroidery foot and lower (or cover) the feed-dogs. Attach the embroidery hoop to the fabric sandwich, then following the technique described on page 126, sew around the outlines of all the circles, stopping at intervals to alter the position of the embroidery hoop. Remove all pins.

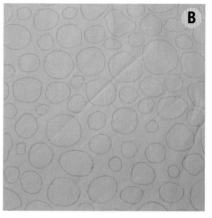

6 When the circle outlines have been sewn, fill in the gaps between them with free-style embroidery using a random pattern **C** . Try to ensure that the 'density' of the sewn thread is the same throughout, otherwise it will look uneven. You may keep the embroidery hoop on for this stage or, if you prefer, it can be removed, now that the circle outlines have been sewn. Photo **D** shows the finished embossed fabric.

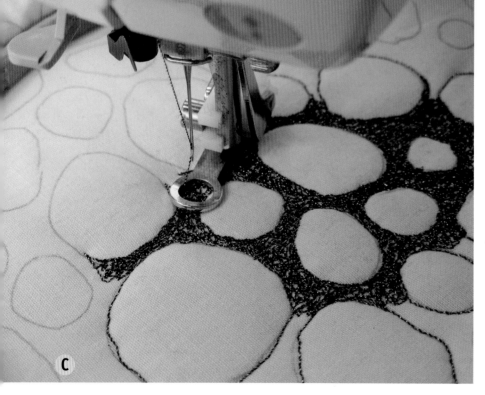

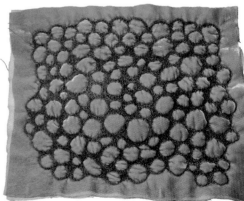

Construction

7 Trim away any excess wadding and scrap fabric from the edges, as close to the stitching as you can, but leave the top velvet layer in place. This simply removes unnecessary bulk.

8 Place your piece of lining material on top of your embossed velvet and, with right sides together, sew the edges all the way around, apart from a gap of approximately 6 in (15 cm) along one edge.

9 Turn it inside out through the gap, so that the right sides are now on the outside. Hand-sew the gap closed. Your lined embossed velvet fabric is now ready for making into the bag. Place it to one side while constructing the handle-bands and tabs.

10 To make the handles, take the spare piece of (un-embossed) velvet that was cut from your original length of fabric, and cut from it four rectangles, each measuring $4 \times 1^5/_8$ in (10×4 cm). Taking one of these, fold it in half lengthways, right sides together, and stitch around one long side and one short side  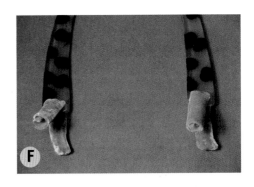 **E**. Turn this inside out through the gap at the remaining end, so that the right sides are on the outside. Press flat. Repeat with the other three. Insert each of these four handle-tabs through the slots in the bottoms of the handles **F**.

Note: *Depending on what sort of handles you have bought, you may have to adjust the width of the handle-tabs to fit through the holes in the handles.*

11 To make the handle-bands, cut four pieces – two for each handle-band – from your remaining piece of un-embossed velvet, each piece measuring $10^1/_4 \times 2^3/_8$ in (2×6 cm). Then cut four pieces of fusible interfacing, each measuring $8 \times 1^9/_{16}$ in (20×4 cm), one for each handle-band section. Iron the interfacing onto the wrong side of each of the four pieces of velvet, allowing a gap around the edges for seams.

12 Take two of the handle-band rectangles and place one on top of the other, right sides together. In between these, place the handle-tabs, still threaded, through the handles. The handle-tabs should protrude beyond the edge of the handle-band rectangles and the handles should come through the opposite sides of the rectangles **G**. Pin in place securely and tack.

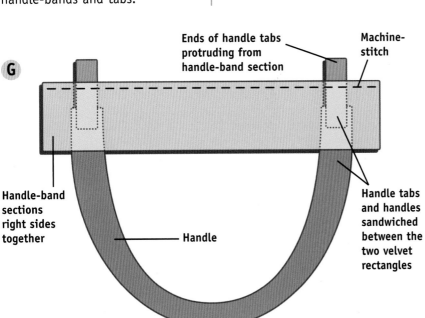

G

Ends of handle tabs protruding from handle-band section

Machine-stitch

Handle-band sections right sides together

Handle

Handle tabs and handles sandwiched between the two velvet rectangles

13 Sew along the top seam, taking care to keep the ends of the handles away from the sewing-machine needle.

14 Fold down each side of the handle-band – so that the wrong sides are together – and top-stitch along the top edge 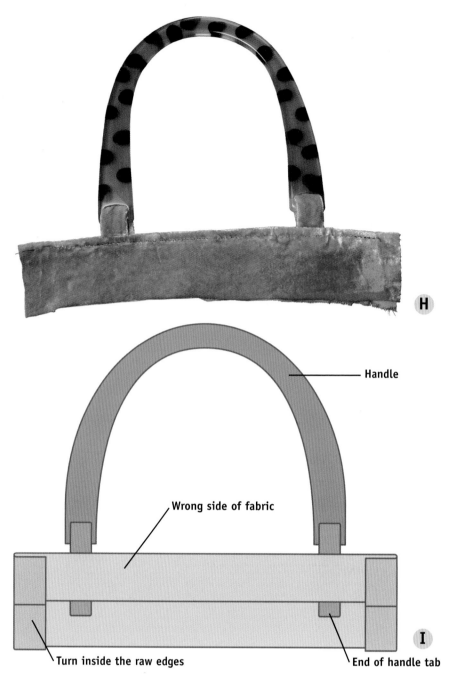 . Repeat the last three steps with the remaining pieces.

15 Turn under the raw edges of each of the shorter edges of your handle-bands so that each one measures 8in (30 cm) in length, making sure that the handle ends are equidistant from each end. Your handle-bands (with handles attached) are now ready to stitch to the main body of the bag.

H

Handle

Wrong side of fabric

Turn inside the raw edges

End of handle tab

I

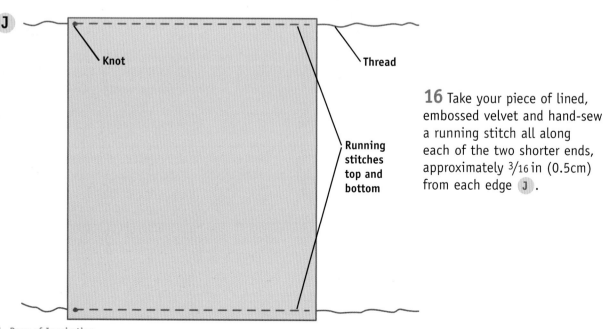

J

Knot

Thread

Running stitches top and bottom

16 Take your piece of lined, embossed velvet and hand-sew a running stitch all along each of the two shorter ends, approximately $3/16$ in (0.5cm) from each edge.

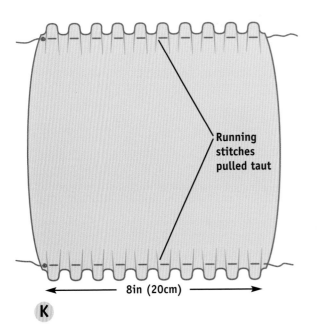

Running stitches pulled taut

8in (20cm)

K

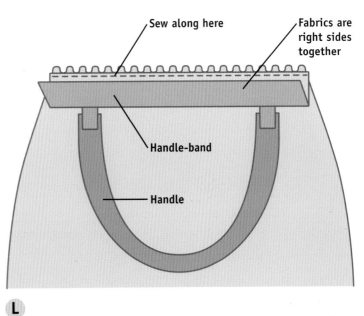

Sew along here

Fabrics are right sides together

Handle-band

Handle

L

17 Draw the threads up to gather each end to a length of 8 in (20 cm). Secure the thread **K**.

18 Take one handle-band and place it right sides together along one gathered edge of the velvet fabric **L**. Pin and tack securely in place, then machine-stitch. (If you want the handle-bands to be really stiff, you can also insert some stiffening fabric.)

19 Fold the other side of the handle-band over, turn under the raw edge and hand-sew neatly in place to the lining **M**.

Note: *Depending on the type of fastening you choose, you may need to attach these before hand-sewing the edge in place. Photo* **M** *shows a magnetic fastener already attached.*

20 Attach the other handle-band to the other end of the fabric in the same way.

21 Fold the fabric in half, right sides together, aligning the handle-bands so that they fall exactly one on top of the other. Pin and tack the side seams then machine-stitch as far as the edges of the handle-bands.

22 Turn inside out so that the bag now has the right sides on the outside. If you have not already attached magnetic fasteners, attach the press-stud fastenings to the inside of the handle-bands.

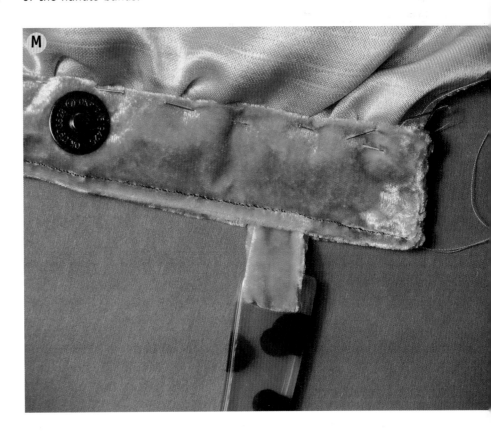

M

Pink Extravaganza

A Bag using the Slashed Layers Technique

This bag combines vibrant colour with tactile softness. Attention-grabbing pink inspired the choice for the main fabric, which, together with the other bright colours, creates a stunning visual effect. At the same time, the softness of the velvet is further enhanced by the fluffy texture that is created by the 'slashed layers' technique.

Materials

- Six pieces of fabric for the layers, each 21 × 13 in (53 × 33 cm). (Note that the weave should be parallel to the edges of the fabric – unlike the example in 'Special Effects' on page 133 – as the cuts are to be diagonal.) Here the top layer is pink velvet, while the lower layers are all thin fabrics, the bottom one being gold-coloured

- An additional piece of fabric measuring 21 × 13 in (53 × 33 cm) for the lining
- A length of gilt chain for the strap measuring approximately 51 in (130 cm)
- About 120 in (300 cm) of feathery ribbon yarn, also for the strap
- A magnetic fastener
- Machine cotton

- A temporary fabric marker
- Optional: A piece of lining material measuring 14¹/₂ × 8 in (37 × 20 cm) for the pocket
- Optional: Decorative button
- Optional: Decorative feathers

It is advisable to choose fabrics that are, in the main, fairly thin, otherwise your sewing machine may have difficulty. Also, use a fine needle in your sewing machine if you are working with a lot of layers. Here, six layers of fabric have been used, but you could create a similar effect with fewer. Experiment with different fabrics and numbers of layers to discover the effects that may be achieved.

See **Special Effects, Slashed Layers**, pages 133–135

Instructions

Preparing the fabric

1 Place your six layers of fabric one on top of the other 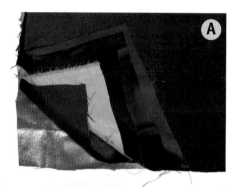. Pin and tack these layers together so that they cannot slide about.

2 Sew a series of diagonal parallel lines about 3/8 in (1 cm) apart across the entire fabric . (The lines need to be diagonal so that they run diagonally across the weave of the fabric, not parallel to it.) The distance between each line is not critical but for a pleasing effect you should try to make them equal (you can use a temporary fabric marker pen if this helps). Photo  shows the layers of fabric after all the lines have been sewn.

3 With small, sharp scissors, carefully cut between each pair of parallel lines through all the layers except the last . It is important you don't cut through the bottom layer or up to the very edge of the fabric; you need to leave a gap of at least 5/8 in (1.5 cm) between your cut line and the edge of the fabric. This cutting procedure takes a time, especially if you have lots of layers. You may be able to cut through the top five layers in one go, or you may want to cut through just two or three at a time. Photo  shows the fabric after all the lines have been cut.

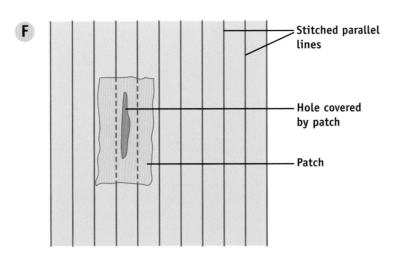

Stitched parallel
lines

Hole covered
by patch

Patch

Tip

*If you do happen to cut through
the bottom layer of fabric (easily
done!), you can repair this by
turning the fabric layers over so
that the bottom layer is positioned
uppermost, and spraying lightly
around the hole with temporary
fabric adhesive. You can then stick
a small patch of the same fabric
over the top, so that the sides of
the patch extend beyond the two
adjacent 'tramlines'* **F** *, turn the
fabric the right way up and then
carefully machine-stitch over the
two tramlines that are in the area
of the patch, to secure it in place.*

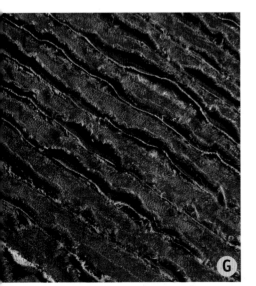

4 Now you need to distress the
fabric. To achieve the fluffy look
along the cut edges, which is
characteristic of this effect (and
has led to the name *faux chenille*)
you need to rub the material
between your fingers and thumb
to cause the edges to fray
slightly. (They cannot fray away
completely because you have
made the cuts diagonally to the
direction of the weave.) You can
be even rougher if you wish, by
brushing the top of the fabric
with a fine wire brush. Washing it
will help to fluff up the edges,
too. Photo **G** shows in detail the
surface of the fabric after it has
been distressed.

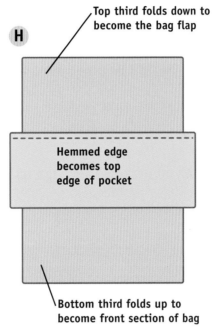

Top third folds down to
become the bag flap

Hemmed edge
becomes top
edge of pocket

Bottom third folds up to
become front section of bag

Construction

5 Take your small piece of lining
material for the pocket, measuring
$14^{1}/_{2} \times 8$ in (37×20 cm), and
hem one of the long sides
allowing about $^{5}/_{8}$ in (1.5 cm) for
the seam. This side will become
the top edge of the pocket.

6 Now take the larger piece of
lining material and place it on top
of your prepared fabric, right sides
together. Pin it in three or four
places to secure it roughly then
fold the entire piece into thirds,
with the lining on the inside, in
order to determine the exact
positioning of the pocket. In this
design the pocket is wide and
deep, extending the full width of
the inside of the bag. The bottom
edge of the pocket piece should
extend about $^{5}/_{8}$ in (1.5 cm) below
where the bottom of the bag
interior will be. The top edge
should come just below the top of
the front edge of the bag, so that
when the bag is opened, the top
of the pocket is just slightly
below the opening. The side edges
of the pocket piece should extend
a little way beyond the sides of
the lining.

7 When you have determined the
position of the pocket, pin and
tack it to the main lining fabric
(wrong side of pocket to right
side of lining fabric), making sure
that the hemmed edge is facing
inwards towards the lining **H** .

8 Now place your lining fabric once more on top of the prepared fabric, wrong sides together, and machine-stitch all around the edge, leaving a gap of about 5 in (12cm) through which you can turn it inside out.

9 Turn the fabric inside out so that the right sides of the prepared fabric and the lining material are facing outwards, and the pocket is firmly in place on the upper side of the lining fabric ⓘ. Close the gap by turning in the edge of the lining material and sewing it by hand to the rest of the fabric ⓙ.

10 Roughly fold the fabric into thirds again (with the lining on the inside) and, with a temporary fabric marker, mark on the lining fabric the position of the bottom of the bag. To complete the pocket open it out and hem-stitch the bottom edge to the place on the lining which represents the bottom of the interior of the bag.

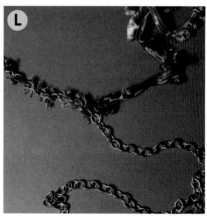

11 Fold the bottom third of the fabric up to form the main body of the bag and machine-stitch in place ⓚ.

12 Make the strap by taking your length of gilt chain and weaving through the links a length of feathery ribbon yarn ⓛ. You may need to do this two or three times to achieve a satisfactory effect.

Note: *If you want to attach a magnetic fastener, you will need to do so before you finish sewing the lining to the main fabric.*

13 Hand-sew the chain to the sides of the bag **M** .

14 If you have not already attached a magnetic fastener to your bag, a press-stud fastener may now be fitted.

15 Optional: You may also affix a decorative button to the top of the bag flap **N** .

16 Optional: For some further embellishment, bind a few decorative feathers together at their stems with gold thread **O** and hand-sew them to the top right-hand corner of the bag flap. In this example, a cluster of gold seed beads has also been added **P** .

Dream Wedding

A Drawstring Bag with Ribbons and Braids

This is a very simple bag to make and it can, in fact, be made in just an afternoon. It is also delightful to decorate, as you can really have fun, sewing on all manner of ribbon remnants and braids. It lends itself well to a variety of colours and fabrics, but I chose a cream heavy satin and decorated it with cream and white embellishments, as I was inspired by the icing on a wedding cake!

Materials

- One piece of heavy cream satin measuring 32×14 in (81×35 cm)
- One piece of cream silk of the same dimensions for the lining
- 80 in (200 cm) cream twisted cord
- An assortment of cream and white ribbons, lace and braids
- Machine cotton

If you choose fabric other than satin for the bag then it is wise not to select a thick fabric as it will be too bulky to easily gather up along the drawstring band.

Instructions

Preparing the fabric | Construction

1 Cut out two pieces of satin according to the shape and dimensions that are shown in diagram **A**. Photo **B** shows one of the pieces cut out.

2 With right sides together, machine-stitch all the way around, with a seam allowance of 3/8 in (1 cm) and leaving the opening at the top unstitched.

3 Keeping the two pieces right sides together, turn down to the outside a 5/8 in (1.5 cm) hem all the way around the top opening. Machine-stitch in place.

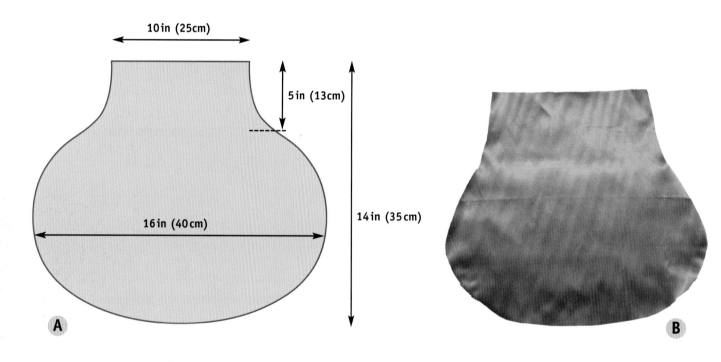

10 in (25 cm)

5 in (13 cm)

16 in (40 cm)

14 in (35 cm)

A

B

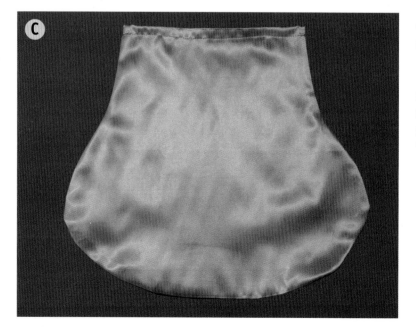

C

4 Next, turn the right sides to the outside **C** .

5 Fold the top edge of the bag down to the inside, all the way around, to a depth of at least 1 1/2 in (4 cm). Pin and tack.

6 Machine-stitch along the very edge of the turned-down rim, from the inside  D.

7 Now machine-stitch another line, parallel to the last, $5/8$ in (1.5 cm) higher, so that you are sewing on top of the line of stitches that you previously sewed in step 3. These two 'tramlines' will form the channel through which the cord will run.

8 With a small pair of fine-pointed scissors, carefully cut the side-seam stitches just between the tramlines. Do this on both sides.

9 Cut your cord into two lengths, each 40 in (102 cm) long. Take one piece, attach a safety pin to one end and feed it through one of the gaps you have just made in the side seam E. Feed it right the way around, until it emerges through the same hole at which it entered. Remove the safety pin.

10 Repeat with the other piece of cord, but this time thread it through the opposite side F. Tie each pair of ends together in a neat knot.

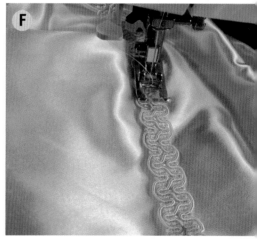

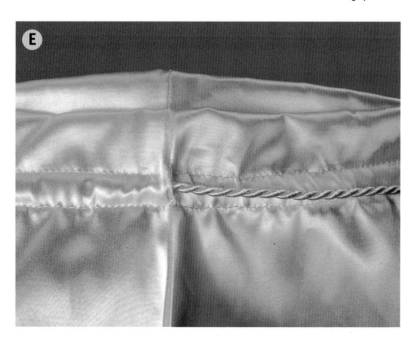

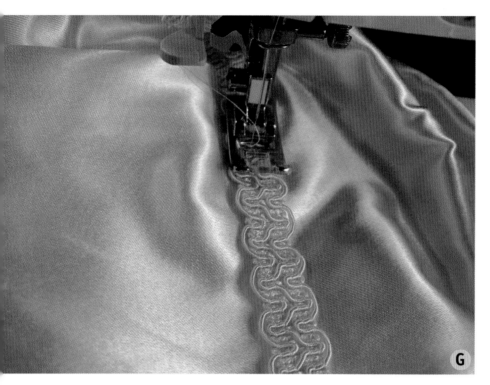

11 Now it is time to sew onto the outside of your bag all the lovely pieces of ribbon, braid and lace which you have selected. You can either machine-stitch these in place (G), or sew them on by hand. Photo (H) shows the bag after it has been decorated.

Note: *An alternative method would be to sew all the ribbons and braid onto each piece of fabric before sewing them together. This makes it easier to sew them on, but from a design perspective it is better to decide where to put the different pieces after the bag has been made up, so that you can see the overall shape.*

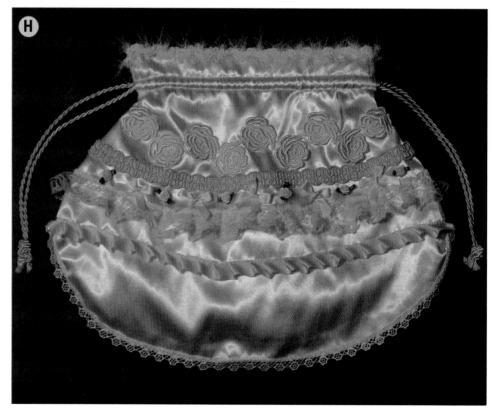

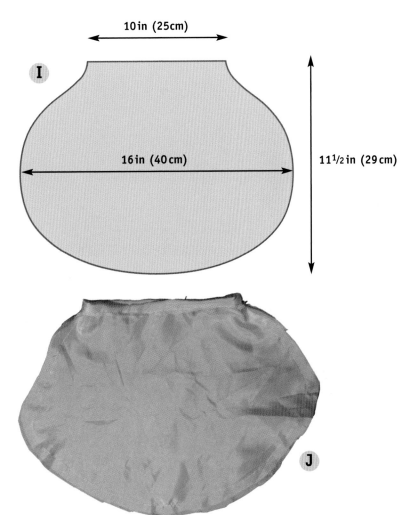

I

10 in (25cm)

16 in (40 cm)

11½ in (29 cm)

12 To make the lining, cut two pieces of silk according to the dimensions given in diagram **I**.

13 With right sides together, machine-stitch all the way round, with a seam allowance of ³⁄₈ in (1 cm) and leaving the opening. Now turn down a hem of ⁵⁄₈ in (1.5 cm) around the opening **J**.

14 Place the lining (inside out) inside the bag, matching up the side seams. Pin the neck of the lining so that its top edge is just below the bottom edge of the cord channel. Hand-stitch in place as shown in photo **K**.

J

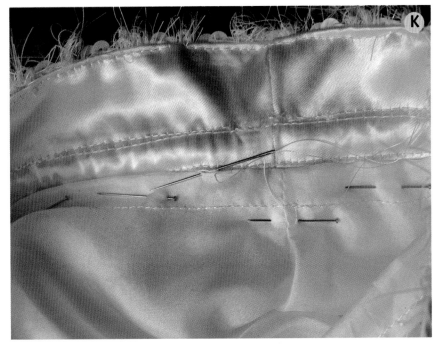

K

15 Finally, to secure the bottom of the lining in place, carefully hand-sew a few stitches at intervals, to join the bottom seam of the lining to the bottom seam of the bag.

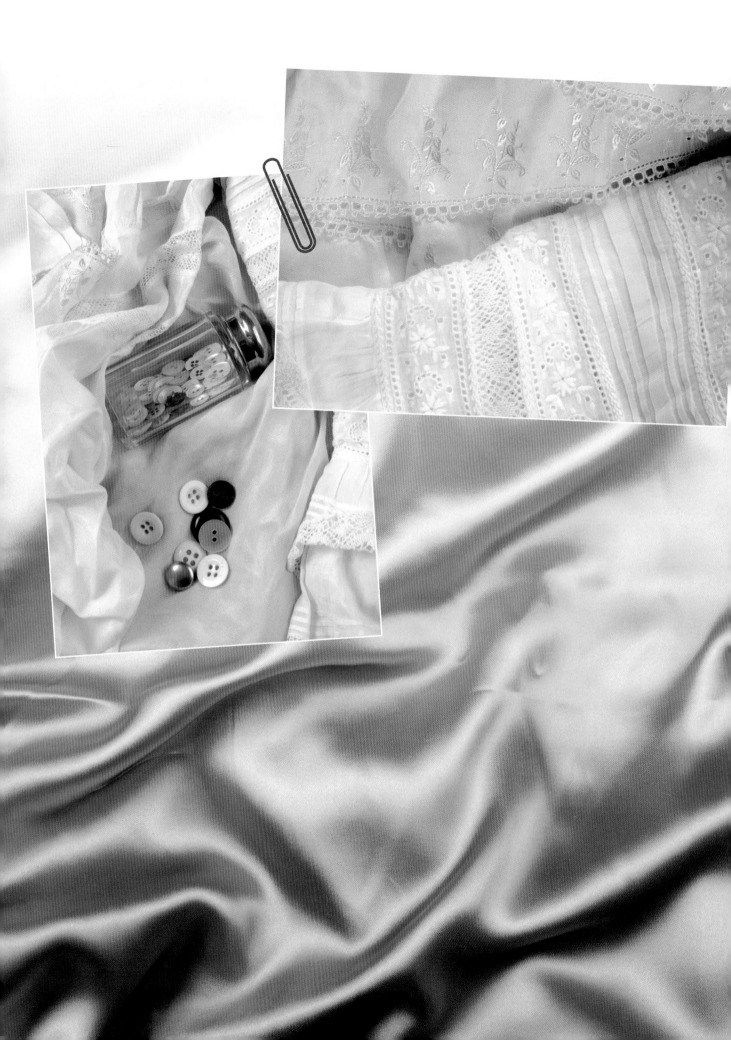

Granny's Treasure

A Bag with a Metal Frame Handle

The starting point for this bag was the beautiful antique-effect metal frame handle, reminiscent of a bygone era. I wanted to echo this 'antique' feel with the overall design. So, for the main fabric I used a soft viscose velvet, printed in muted pastel colours, and decorated it with sequins and small antique mother-of-pearl buttons. I chose a rich mauve satin for the lining.

Materials

- Printed velvet measuring 28 × 11 in (71 × 28 cm)
- Lining material of the same dimensions
- One metal fixed-frame handle measuring 8½ × 3 in (22 × 7.5 cm)
- Large assortment of buttons, beads and sequins
- Machine cotton
- Strong thread of a suitable colour to match the velvet and the lining material (as it will show on both sides)

For this design, the dimensions of the fabric are determined by the size of the jaws of the fixed-frame handle. To measure this you need to open out the jaws of your handle so that they are flat, then measure the perimeter all the way round. This length needs to be equal to (or slightly less than) the total perimeter of the the top opening of the bag. Here, the jaws measured 26¾ in (68 cm). I needed to add on some extra for seam allowances, plus a bit extra again. In this case ¾ in (2 cm) was added altogether, making a total length of 27½ in (70 cm). It is better to err on the generous side – if the 'mouth' of the bag is slightly bigger than the metal jaws, this will not matter, since the fabric can be gently eased to fit the jaws, but if the 'mouth' is too small, it cannot be stretched to fit.

Instructions

Preparing the fabric

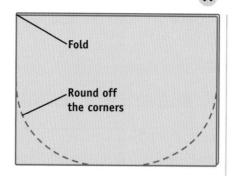

1 Take your length of velvet fabric, fold it in half widthways and round off the corners **A**.

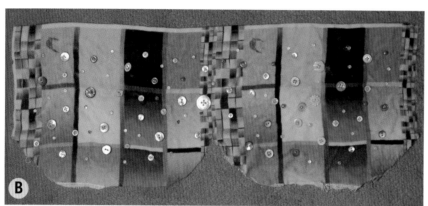

2 Hand-sew onto the fabric your assortment of buttons, beads and sequins. You can sew on as many or as few as you wish, either in a random fashion (as in this example) or in patterns and lines. You may wish to add further embellishments to the fabric after the bag has been made up, but for sewing on the bulk of the buttons, beads and sequins, it is best done at this stage while the fabric remains unattached. Photo **B** shows the fabric shaped at the corners and with most of the buttons and sequins sewn in place.

Construction

3 With right sides together, fold the fabric in half widthways and sew around the open sides, leaving the top open. Now turn the right sides out **C**.

4 Take your lining material and shape the corners in the same way as you did for the velvet. Then, right sides together, fold in half widthways and sew around the open edges, except for the top to form a bag identical in size and shape to the velvet one.

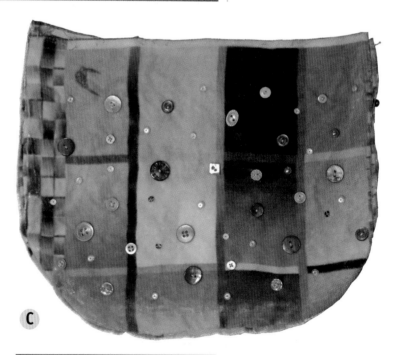

5 Keeping the lining 'bag' inside out, slip it over its velvet counterpart so that the top edges are aligned. Pin the top edge of the lining fabric to the top edge of the velvet **D**. Tack the edge and remove the pins.

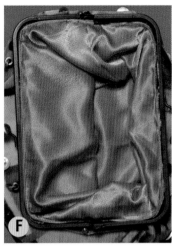

6 Machine-stitch all around this edge, leaving a gap of about 4in (10 cm), then turn the bag right sides out through the gap. Now hand-sew the gap together. Photo E shows the lining attached to the inside of the bag.

7 Now open out the 'mouth' of the bag (i.e. the top opening) and place the edges inside the opened jaws of the fixed-frame handle F. It is important you align the side seams of the bag exactly with the side hinges of the metal frame G.

8 Roughly tack the top opening of the bag to the metal frame to secure it in place H. Then with some strong thread in a colour that matches both the velvet and the satin, neatly double-stitch the top opening of the bag to the metal frame, using the holes in the frame. Remove the tacking stitches. Photo I shows the bag stitched in place onto the frame.

9 Optional: If you wish you can now add further decorative embellishments, such as braids, more sequins and any other pretty motifs.

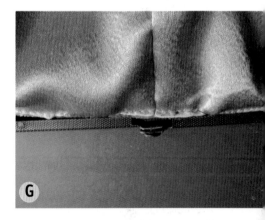

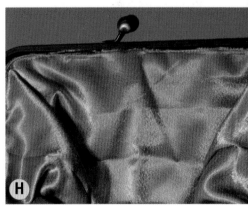

Luscious Lips

A Bag with a Zipped Opening

This one's just for fun. It is quick and easy to construct and will make you smile!

Materials

- Red satin measuring about 27 × 17 in (68 × 43 cm)
- Wadding of the same dimensions
- Fusible interfacing of the same dimensions
- Red satin for the strap measuring 40 × 3 in (102 × 8 cm)
- One red zip measuring 9½ in (24 cm)
- Red machine cotton

Although this bag could be made in any other fabric, if it is going to be in the shape of lips then red satin or silk is the best choice.

Instructions

Preparing the fabric

1 From the large piece of red satin, cut out four lip shapes using the template on the facing page. One of these cut-outs is illustrated in photo **A**.

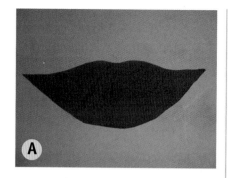

2 From your wadding cut out four identical lip shapes. Now, using fusible interfacing, iron on a piece of wadding to each of the four pieces of red satin **B**.

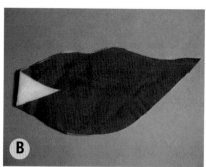

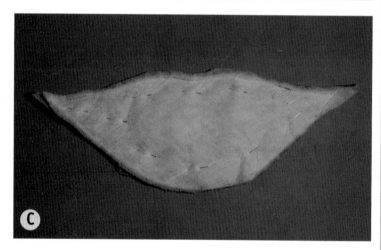

3 Take one pair of shapes and place them satin sides together. Pin all around the edge then machine-stitch, leaving a gap of approximately 2⅜ in (6 cm) at the bottom unstitched **C**.

4 Now turn the right sides out through the gap and hand-sew up the gap.

5 Machine-stitch a line across the centre to demarcate the two lips **D**. Repeat with the other pair. You will now have the two halves of the bag, one for each side.

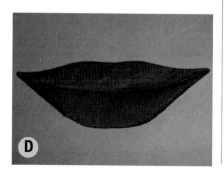

Construction

6 Place the two halves of the bag side by side with the zip in between, as shown in photo **E**. Move the zip so that it is in the centre and pin it to one of the halves.

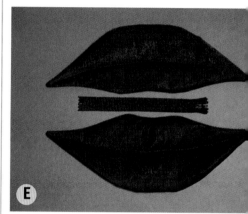

7 Using a sewing machine, top-stitch the top edge of one half of the bag to one side of the zip **F**.

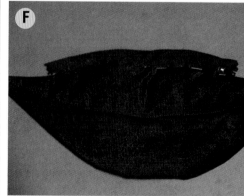

8 To make the strap, take the allocated piece of satin, fold it in half lengthways and then top-stitch all the way round, including the two ends **G**.

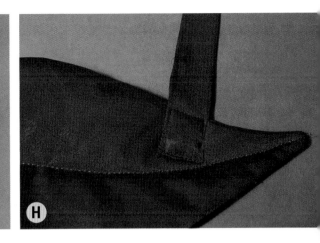

9 Top-stitch one end of the strap to one half of the bag, as shown in photo **H**. Now attach the other end of the strap to the other end of the same side, making sure you don't twist the strap as you go.

10 Now top-stitch the other side of the zip to the remaining half of the bag **I**. Your two halves are now joined together at the top by the zip **J**.

11 To finish, fold the sides down so that they are exactly aligned then pin and top-stitch carefully all around the edge **K**.

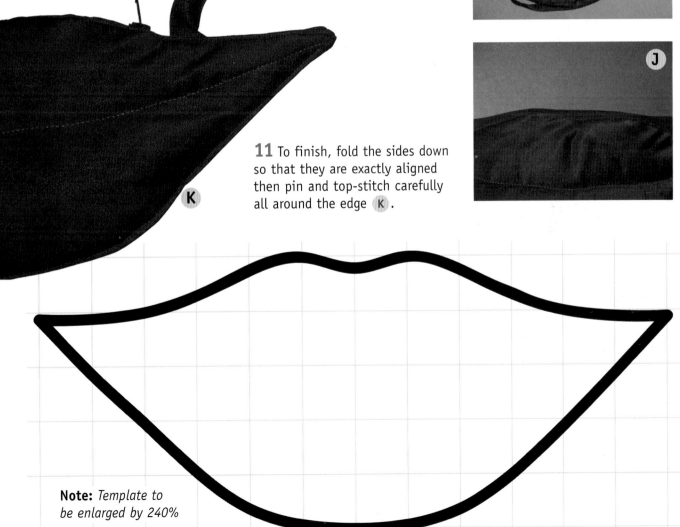

Note: *Template to be enlarged by 240%*

Project Preparation

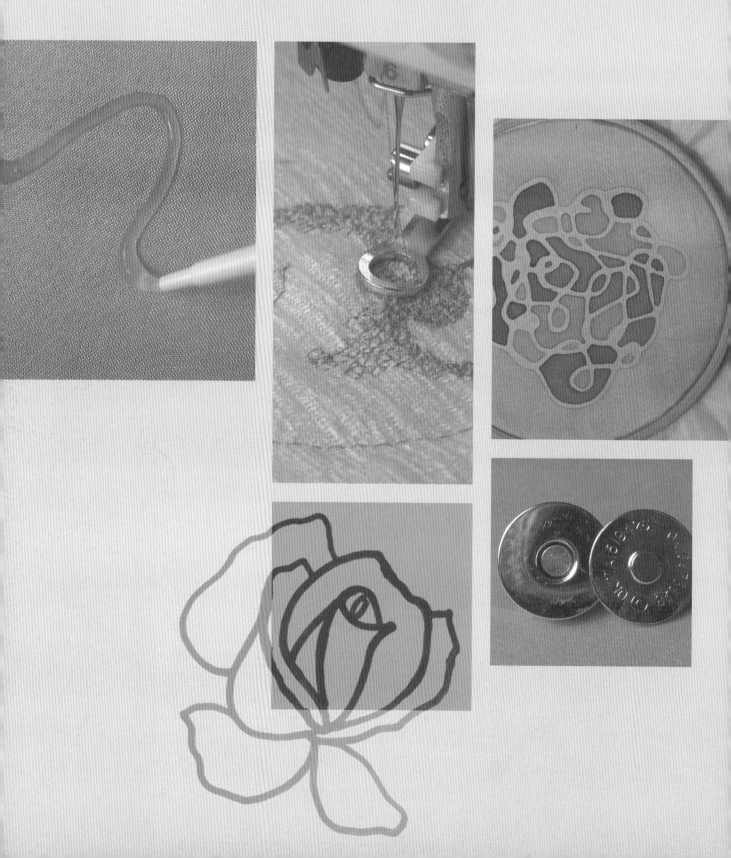

Materials and Equipment

Nowadays there is a huge variety of beautiful fabrics, threads and yarns to choose from: some made from natural fibres, others synthetic. Both natural and synthetic materials have their advantages and can be utilized in different ways.

Recent years have also seen the development of materials designed specifically for those interested in textile art of different kinds. This chapter summarizes a few of those most useful in the creation of decorative bags. The majority of these items can be bought in either haberdashery stores or good hobby/craft shops. Some are available through mail order (see listings on pages 170).

Sewing machine

Although it is possible to make bags entirely by hand-sewing, it would be very time-consuming, so a sewing machine is strongly recommended. A top-of-the-range model is not necessary – any basic sewing machine will do, even very cheap ones usually have a few basic embroidery stitches, such as satin-stitch, which is useful to have. The most important thing is that it should be reliable.

Fabric Ⓐ

This is the starting point for most projects, so a good selection of fabric is essential. When making decorative evening bags the most stunning effects are produced from those really sumptuous fabrics, such as silk, satin, velvet, organza and chiffon.

Ⓐ

Decorative items B

It is useful to keep a collection of interesting buttons, sequins and beads of all shapes, sizes and colours, pieces of ribbon, braid and lace, feathers, and even shells. These can all be stored fairly easily. By stock-piling in this way, you will not only be saving yourself money, you will also be saving time: it is much easier and quicker to have a rummage through your own supplies than have to go out and buy something specially.

Velvets (both cotton and synthetic) have a richness of tone as well as lovely tactile qualities; silk, when dyed, can hold wonderful vivid hues; satin has a gorgeous glossiness, which can be enhanced by quilting techniques; chiffon has an airy lightness ideal for making trims, flowers and other embellishments, while organza has a glitzy sheen, which adds panache to any design.

Unfortunately, all of these fabrics can be expensive to buy. However, only small quantities are usually needed – even tiny pieces of organza or satin added as a trim here and there, together with a few sequins, perhaps, can provide added sparkle. A really good way to obtain fabrics is to buy them from jumble sales and car-boot sales. At such places it is easy to purchase second-hand items of clothing in good condition, extremely cheaply; whole dresses, blouses, skirts and jackets in the most wonderful fabrics can be bought and cut up when needed. By gathering such items over a period of time you can have a permanent store of beautiful fabrics at your fingertips. Also, instead of getting rid of clothes you no longer wear, hang on to that old silk blouse, velvet jacket or chiffon scarf and add them to your fabric store.

Threads c

You can't have too many different types of thread, and there are plenty to choose from. Ordinary machine cotton is useful for all the basic sewing jobs, for example, in constructing the basic bags, but there are some beautiful metallic threads available, which, when used as top-stitching or satin-stitch around an edge, can significantly enhance the overall visual effect. It is important to check, though, which metallic threads are suitable for machine sewing and which are not. Some are designed only for hand-sewing. If you often use metallic thread it is worth buying a sewing-machine needle that is especially designed for use with it. This will help to prevent it tangling or snapping, which can occasionally happen with some metallic threads.

Wadding D

This is an extremely useful item, and almost all the bags illustrated in this book have had wadding incorporated – it helps to give them some 'substance' as well as providing the fabric with a nice soft spongy feel. It is also an essential material when quilting, a technique that can be used to good advantage in many diverse ways. There are different types of wadding – they tend to vary in smoothness and thickness – so it is worth having a look at the various types to decide which best suits your purpose.

Fusible interfacing D

This is another invaluable item and, again, nearly all the bags shown in this book have fusible interfacing used somewhere in their construction. It is not essential but it saves a lot of time, since it can be a quick and useful alternative to sewing. There are various different types on the market, sometimes bearing the brand name Bond-a-web, Thermoweb or Heat 'n' Bond. The most common forms consist of paper with a coating of special adhesive on one side. The paper is usually placed on top of the fabric with the adhesive side in contact with the 'wrong' side of the fabric and it is then ironed on. After leaving it to cool for a few minutes, the paper is peeled away from the fabric, leaving the adhesive layer bonded to the fabric. At this point another piece of fabric can be placed on top, wrong side down, and ironed on. The adhesive melts and bonds the two fabrics together. It is particularly useful for attaching motifs to fabric, as it removes the necessity for fiddly sewing.

Water-soluble fabric

This is a marvellous material. Again, there are numerous types available, sometimes bearing the brand names 'Ario', 'Romeo', or 'Avalon'. They all have one thing in common: they dissolve away when immersed in water. They are used as a support material when doing machine embroidery on thin fabrics to prevent the fabric from puckering and becoming distorted during the sewing process. Fabrics that are fairly stiff anyway, such as thick cotton or linen, are not a problem, but when doing free-style embroidery, satin-stitch, or similar, on fine fabrics such as silk or thin cotton, the shape will distort unless the fabric is supported in some way. If the fabric is large enough, an embroidery hoop can be used instead, but if a small piece of fabric is being sewn (a motif, for example), a hoop is not an option. That is where water-soluble fabric is essential, as your piece of silk, or other fabric, can be pinned to it and sewn easily, as it will be well supported by the water-soluble fabric underneath. When the sewing is complete, it is immersed in water and the water-soluble fabric dissolves instantly. Magic! It is also useful for producing lacy effects with free-style embroidery. By sewing directly onto the water-soluble fabric, an intricate stitched design can be produced. The water-soluble fabric can then be dissolved leaving only the stitching.

Tearable fabric ⓔ

Sometimes sold under the brand name of Stitch 'n' Tear, this is a useful alternative to water-soluble fabric for those occasions when you don't want to expose your item to water. This is a stiff, perforated fabric which can be used as a backing for thin fabrics when doing machine embroidery, just in the same way as water-soluble fabric. The difference is that it is designed to be torn away from the stitching after the sewing is complete.

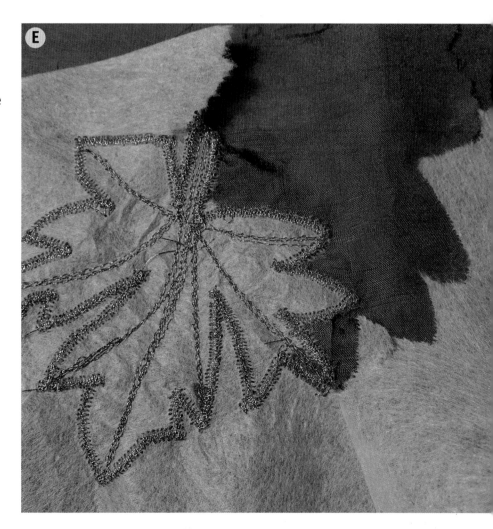

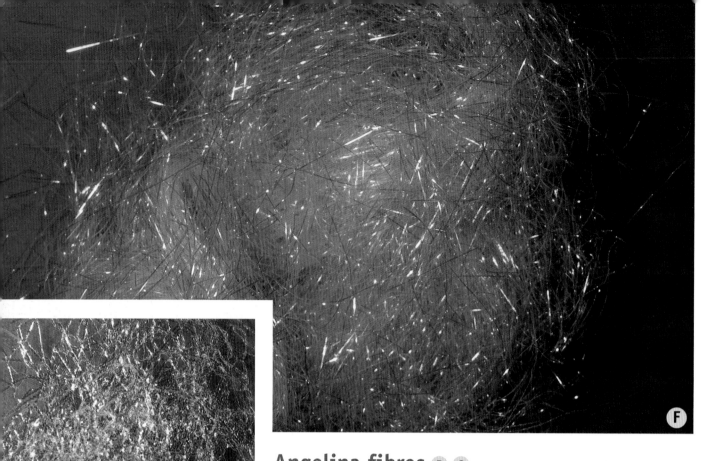

Angelina fibres F G

These are fine, glittery, synthetic fibres similar to those you might use to decorate a Christmas tree. When exposed to heat they melt. By putting a small quantity of Angelina fibres between two pieces of baking parchment and ironing them, they will melt and fuse into a flat, glittery mesh G which can be used in many ways for decorating fabrics. One common way of using these is to iron them between two pieces of fine chiffon (a 'chiffon sandwich'), whereupon the Angelina fibres will melt and you will be left with a double layer of chiffon through which you can see the glittery fibres. This can then form the basis for a motif which can be cut and stitched, or bonded to fabric.

Fabric paints and crayons

These can be put to good effect when you want to add colour to a specific area of fabric without the colour soaking into the fabric, as dye would do. They come in numerous forms and an almost infinite range of colours. Used sparingly they can be very effective.

Temporary marker pens

These are similar to ordinary felt-tip pens, except that the ink is only temporary. With some forms, the ink is designed to wash out in water, but I find that the most useful types are those with ink that gradually fades away – after an hour or so – on exposure to air. They are invaluable for marking out designs on to fabric prior to sewing, especially when you don't want to get the fabric wet at that stage.

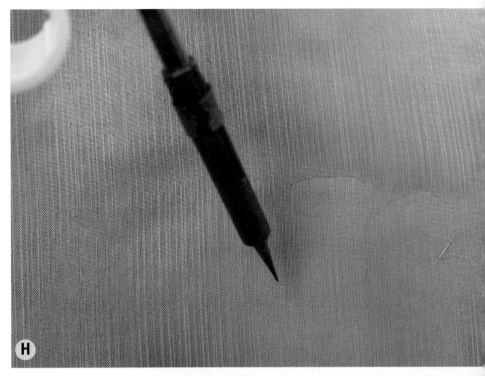

Soldering iron Ⓗ Ⓘ

This may seem like a strange addition to a book on sewing. However, a soldering iron with a fine pointed tip can be very useful for cutting and fusing synthetic fabrics. The tip of the soldering iron simultaneously cuts and fuses the fibres as it is drawn across the fabric. It will also bond two pieces of thin synthetic fabric together (such as organza). Although the fabric must be synthetic – and therefore meltable – you do not want the stitching to melt, so you need to choose your thread carefully. Cotton, rayon and some metallic threads are fine. Not polyester thread, though. If you are in any doubt as to whether fabric or thread will melt, put the tip of the hot soldering iron against a small scrap off the fabric or thread and see what happens. (See Creating Motifs, pages 140–161 and Golden Leaf, pages 57–61.)

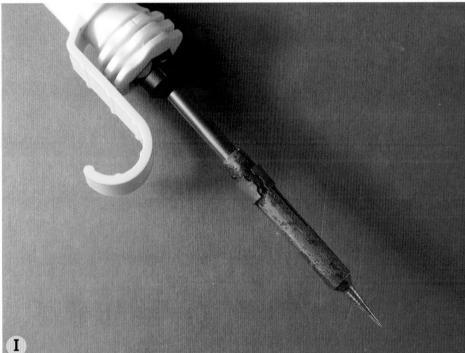

Note: *For a detailed account of how to use this type of soldering iron in relation to fusing fabrics, have a look at* Fusing Fabric *by Margaret Beal. She also supplies the soldering irons.*

Design Considerations

Many of the bag designs in this book are based on shapes and colours found in nature. Inspiration from nature is explored here, too, with suggestions of what to look out for and perhaps use as a starting point for your own designs. It also gives advice on making sure your bag designs are practical.

Finding inspiration

If you ever have difficulty thinking of beautiful and original designs for your bags, you need look no further than your own back garden, at the shapes of leaves, the colours in a butterfly wing, the patterns made by spiders' webs, or the texture in a clump of moss. If you carry a small camera with you, and get into the habit of taking photographs whenever you see something that you think might usefully form the basis of a design, you can build up your own personal image bank. Some examples are illustrated here.

Flowers with simple shapes, such as sunflowers and orchids, can form the basis of lovely designs A and B.

A

B

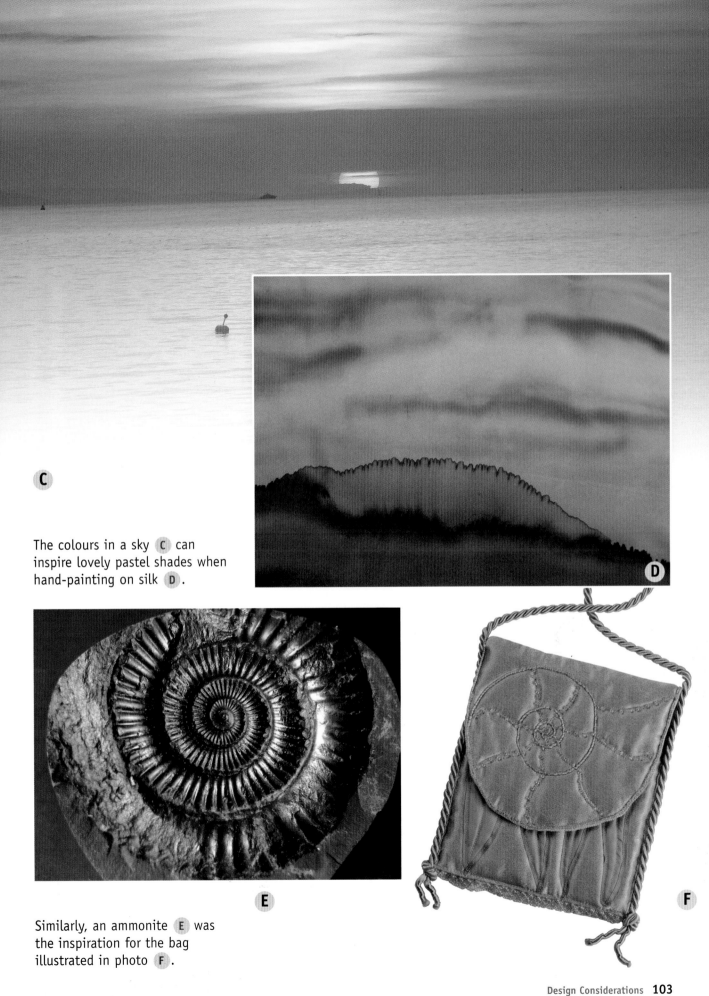

The colours in a sky **C** can inspire lovely pastel shades when hand-painting on silk **D**.

Similarly, an ammonite **E** was the inspiration for the bag illustrated in photo **F**.

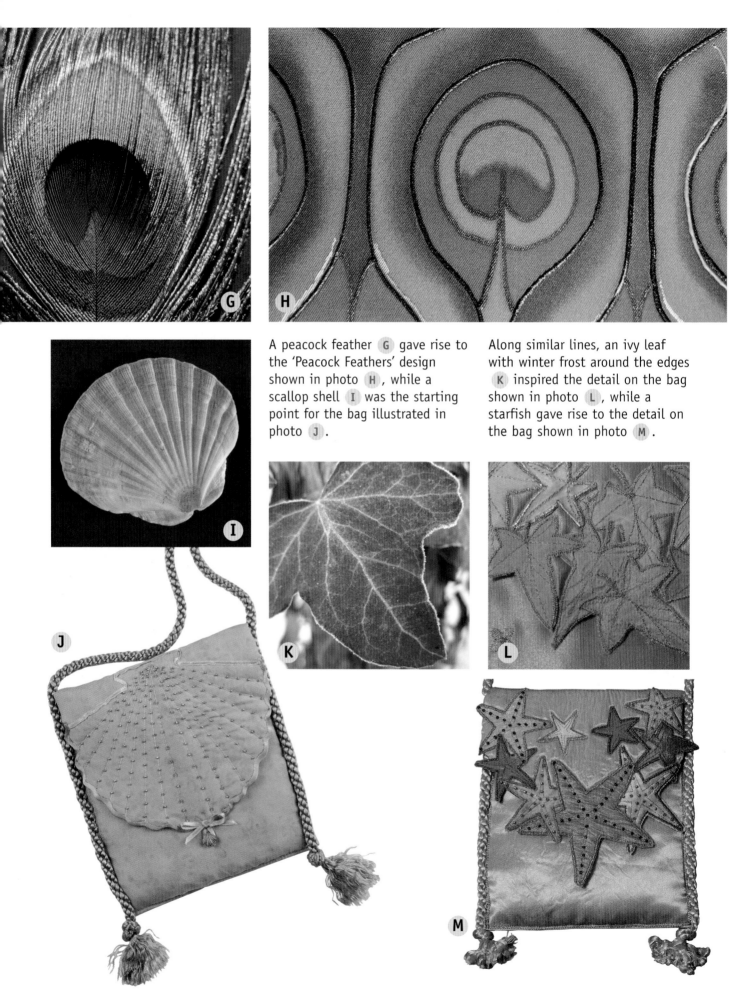

A peacock feather G gave rise to the 'Peacock Feathers' design shown in photo H, while a scallop shell I was the starting point for the bag illustrated in photo J.

Along similar lines, an ivy leaf with winter frost around the edges K inspired the detail on the bag shown in photo L, while a starfish gave rise to the detail on the bag shown in photo M.

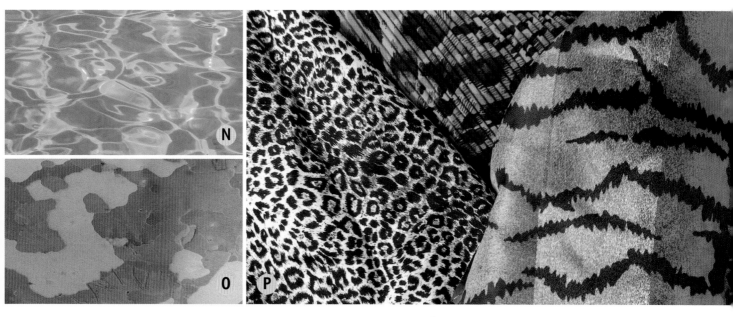

Everywhere you look there are colours, patterns and textures which can be sources of inspiration, such as sunlight reflected from water in a swimming pool N or the bark of a plane tree O .

The fabrics shown in photo P have been inspired by animal prints, and the design for 'Animal', on page 69, also used an animal print as a starting point.

If you do not have a camera, there are numerous other sources from which one can find lovely illustrations of flora and fauna. Books are one obvious source – the local library is a good start, and second-hand book stores if you are on a tight budget. Gardening catalogues and magazines usually have some photographs of plants and flowers, and there are many image banks on the Internet, which has a rich variety of inspirational sources.

From photographs you can begin to build up a few sketches, converting your photographic images into workable designs, as shown in Q . If you lack the confidence to draw, once you have a picture you can always trace it.

However, nature need not be the only source of inspiration. Architectural features, from dry-stone walls to buildings made of glass and steel, medieval houses to an industrial skyline, can all offer ideas in terms of shape, form, colour and texture.

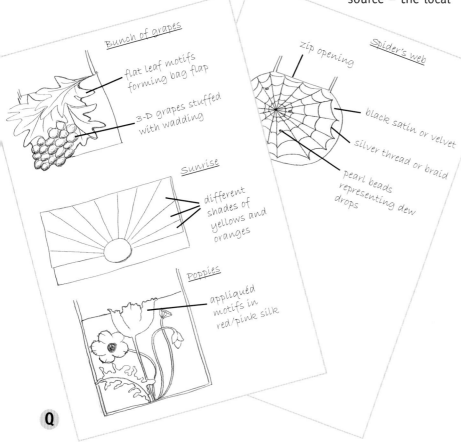

Bunch of grapes
flat leaf motifs forming bag flap
3-D grapes stuffed with wadding

Sunrise
different shades of yellows and oranges

Poppies
appliquéd motifs in red/pink silk

Spider's web
zip opening
black satin or velvet
silver thread or braid
pearl beads representing dew drops

Practicality

Any designer, in whatever field, must strike a balance between form and function, but sometimes one of these is sacrificed for the sake of the other: some chair designs, which look striking but are really uncomfortable to sit on, have sacrificed comfort for style and, at the other extreme, many useful and functional items simply do not sell well because they are ugly. The effective designer must try to marry style with practicality. Handbags are a good example. On the one hand, they must fulfil their purpose as containers, yet at the same time, we want them to be stylish. There is no point creating the most avant-garde and visually stunning handbag if its design makes it difficult to get anything in or out. Don't be tempted to add anything sharp or spiky, either – even if it looks terrific – as it will only get caught on things.

Handles

Handles and fastenings must be considered in the early design stages: do you want a short handle or a shoulder strap? Do you want one handle or two? How should the handle(s) be attached to the main body of the bag? Do you want a flexible handle or a rigid one? Maybe you don't want a handle at all.

One of the simplest ways of adding a shoulder strap is by sewing a length of cord, knotted at each end, down the sides of the bag. This is inexpensive and can be very effective. Many of the bags illustrated in this book have shoulder straps made in this way.

Alternatively, a shoulder strap can be made of the same fabric as the main body of the bag, and can consist of a strip of fabric which runs all the way down the sides of the bag, forming a gusset at the same time.

In a similar way, strips of fabric can be plaited to form a strap R .

A length of gilt chain can be used as a strap, sewn onto the sides of the bag and decorated by weaving ribbon or decorative yarn through the links S and T .

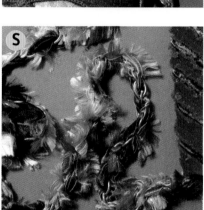

Large beads threaded onto sturdy fishing line can also work well, but bear in mind that beads may not be very comfortable to wear over the shoulder. Clear plastic tubing can be used to good effect when beads or colourful yarns are threaded through.

If you prefer short handles to shoulder straps, these, again, can be made from the same fabric as the bag. Make two fabric tubes, stuff them with wadding and sew them onto the opening of the bag U . Alternatively, you can buy some beautiful rigid handles made from acrylic V and W , or metal 'antique-effect' handles X . Whichever type of handles you choose, they must be incorporated into your design at the initial stages.

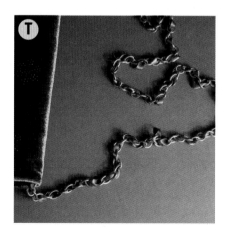

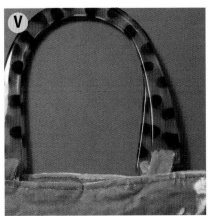

Fastenings

Fastenings are another consideration. Press-stud fasteners come in all shapes, sizes and designs, from the simplest snap fastener **Y**, to a press-stud which has a decorative upper cap **Z**, while magnetic fasteners are very convenient and come in a variety of sizes and colours **AA**. Another option is to use Velcro.

You may prefer to use a button and loop to fasten your bag **BB**, or emulate the bag in photo **CC**, which has a loop of pink ribbon hooked around a small shell-shaped button, mirroring the shape of the 'scallop shell' bag, shown on page 104.

Consider the method of fastening at an early stage in the construction of your bag, because some types of fastener (such as the magnetic ones) need to be inserted between two layers of fabric, which must to be done before the bag is finished. Press-stud fasteners, on the other hand, can be sewn in place at the end. For the smaller projects described in this book I have recommended using press-stud fasteners. For the larger bags, I have suggested magnetic fasteners, but either could be used for any size bag provided they are a suitable size.

Some designs of bag, of course, have a zipped opening (see 'Luscious Lips' on page 91), or a metal handle with clips (see 'Granny's Treasure', left and on page 87), so additional fasteners are not required.

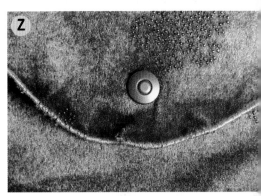

Making the Basic Bag

This bag is used as the basis for most of the designs in this book. It is easy to make, simple to adapt and economical on fabric.

Materials

- A piece of fabric measuring 23 × 16 in (58 × 40 cm)
- Optional: Another piece of the same fabric for the strap measuring 50 × 1³/₁₆ in (127 × 3 cm)
- Optional: A small piece of the same fabric measuring approximately 3³/₁₆ × 2³/₈ in (8 × 6 cm) for the button cover and the button tab
- A length of the same fabric measuring 8¹/₂ × 1³/₁₆ in (21 × 3 cm) for the channel through which the strap will run
- A piece of wadding measuring 23 × 8 in (58 × 20 cm)
- Optional: A piece of fusible interfacing of the same dimensions as the wadding
- Approximately 50 in (125 cm) of cord, about ¹/₄ in (0.5 cm) wide
- Optional: A coverable button measuring approximately ³/₄ in (2 cm) in diameter

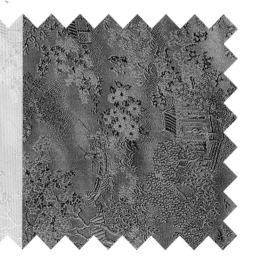

This design essentially consists of a rectangular 'sandwich' of fabric with a layer of wadding in between. The rectangle is folded approximately into thirds and the bottom third stitched, leaving the top third to form the flap that folds over to close the bag. In most designs illustrated in this book it is this flap that forms the principal surface for decoration.

Instructions

Preparing the fabric

1 From your chosen fabric, cut your rectangle measuring approximately 23 × 16 in (58 × 40 cm) . (The precise measurements will depend on the desired size and shape of the finished bag – you may want to adjust these dimensions.)

2 From a length of wadding, cut another rectangle of the same length but half the width, i.e. 23 × 8 in (58 × 20 cm) and then iron the fusible interfacing onto the wadding **B**.

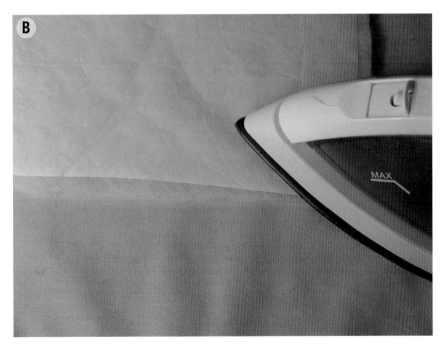

3 Transfer the wadding by further ironing onto the top half of the wrong side of the fabric **C**. Alternatively, if you do not wish to use fusible interfacing, then fold the fabric right sides together lengthways, and pin and tack the wadding to it so that all sides and corners match up **D**.

C

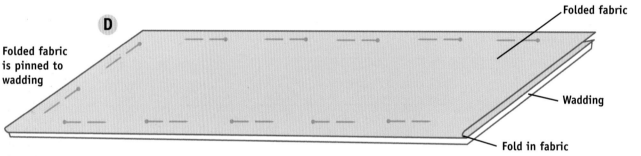

D

Folded fabric is pinned to wadding

Folded fabric

Wadding

Fold in fabric

E

4 Using a plain stitch, sew along two sides of the rectangle, leaving the 'fold' edge and one short side unstitched **E**.

Construction

6 Take the bottom (stitched) end of the rectangle and fold it up so that it rests just over one third of the way up, approximately 7 in (18 cm). Now pin and stitch this in place **G**.

5 Turn this rectangle inside out, taking care to push the two bottom corners out thoroughly (a knitting needle can be used for this). You should now have a rectangular 'sandwich' consisting of fabric right side up on the top and bottom, with a layer of wadding in the middle **F**.

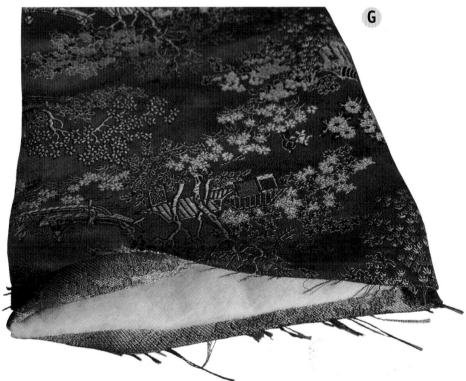

7 Trim the flap of the bag to the desired size and shape. For example, you may wish to keep it rectangular so that its lower edge is parallel to the bottom of the bag, you may wish to curve it up to one side, or perhaps convert it into a semi-circle, depending on your design plans. In this example the lower end of the flap is cut into a pointed shape **H**.

8 Turn the raw edges of the top side of the bag flap over and pin into place . Bring up the underside raw edge and neatly hand-sew this in place, leaving a gap at the pointed end for insertion of the button tab. (This is only necessary if you choose to use this method of fastening. If you prefer to use a press-stud fastener you will not need a button tab. See 'Note' below.)

9 Optional: To make the button tab, cut a rectangular piece of fabric measuring $3^3/_{16} \times {}^2/_3$ in (8×2 cm). Fold this, right sides together, lengthways and stitch the long edges together. Turn this inside out and press. Fold in half and insert the ends into the pointed end of the bag flap.

Note: *In place of a button-and-tab fastening you could use snap fasteners, Velcro, or a loop of ribbon/decorative elastic, sewn onto the bottom of the flap and looped around a button, toggle, bead or other suitable item.*

The important thing is to try, if you possibly can, to choose a method of fastening which is aesthetically pleasing and which relates in some way to the overall design, either in terms of shape, colour or texture.

J

10 Top-stitch all the way around the edge of the bag flap to give it a neat finish J.

11 Optional: If you have inserted a button tab, as just described, you will now want to make your button. For this you will need a 'coverable' button base. These are readily available from most haberdashery suppliers and consist of a top face section and bottom section, which clips into place. In this example the button base is approximately 1 in (2.5cm) in diameter. Cut a circle of fabric just big enough to cover the button face and then fold under its edge and clip the bottom section into place. Fold the bag flap over the front of the bag into its normal position and mark with a pin where the button needs to be. Sew the button into place.

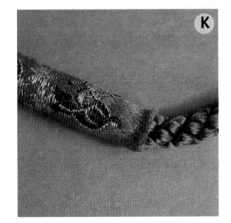

K

12 Next you need to consider how to make the strap or handle, and what length it is to be. You may decide not to have any kind of handle at all, and just leave it as a 'clutch' bag. However, if you do want to have a shoulder strap, a simple method is to use a length of cord. If you wish, you can cover the cord with fabric so that it matches the bag, as described here: Cut a length of fabric approximately $50 \times 1^{3}/_{16}$ in (127×3 cm). With right sides together, fold it in half lengthways and stitch along the long edge. Turn it inside out so that you have a hollow tube. Now cut a piece of cord the same length as your tube of fabric and attach a safety pin to one end. Feed the cord into the tube using the safety pin to guide it through K. When you have fed the cord all the way through to the other end, remove the safety pin and fasten the ends of the cord to the ends of the fabric, with a few neat hand-stitches to hold it in place.

13 The strap is now ready to be attached to your bag, so you must decide where you are going to attach it. One simple method is to sew the two ends of the strap to the sides of the bag, leaving the middle loop free to go over the shoulder. However, you can also fasten the strap to the inside of the bag, by threading it through a channel of fabric sewn on the inside of the base of the flap. If you decide to use this method you will need to do the following.

Cut a piece of fabric that is about 1³/₁₆ in (3 cm) wide, which is approximately 1 in (2.5cm) longer than the width of your bag. In this example it would measure 8³/₁₆ × 1³/₁₆ in (21 × 3 cm). Fold the two short ends inwards by ³/₈ in (1 cm) and stitch. (This should now be the same length as the width of your bag.) Fold under ³/₈ in (1 cm) along the long side of this rectangle of fabric. Pin and sew it to the inside of the base of the bag flap.

Next, feed the strap under this rectangle (having already sewn the two free ends of the strap together) ⓛ. Make sure the join in the strap is inside the channel and therefore concealed. When the strap is in place, turn under the remaining raw edge of the channel and pin it into position. Tack and machine-stitch in place ⓜ. (You will find it easier to use a zipper foot on your sewing machine for this operation, if you have one.)

14 At this stage you may decide that your bag is finished; however, there is no limit to the decorative embellishments that may be added. For example, gathered fabric or ribbon may be stitched along the bottom edge of the bag. Metallic thread may be machine-stitched using a decorative machine-stitch along the edges of the bag. Sequins, beads, shells and feathers may also be added. If you have used a plain fabric for your bag, you may wish to decorate the flap in some way. For this you need to see step 15.

15 If fabric motifs are to be attached, either by hand-stitching or by using iron-on fusible interfacing, then there will be no visible stitching on the underside of the flap. If machine-stitching is to be used as a means of decorating the flap (either as decoration in itself or to attach fabric motifs), then there will be some stitching visible on the underside of the flap. If this stitching is very neat and/or fairly minimal, then this is quite acceptable. However, some stitching techniques create a

veritable 'bird's nest' of untidy threads which would be unsightly. In this case, carefully unpick the stitching that holds the two sides of the flap together or, if you have really thought ahead, then leave the flap section unstitched altogether when you are sewing the inside-out rectangle described in step 2. (Although it does make sense to think ahead and to leave this section unstitched, sometimes it is simply easier to sew all the way round the three sides of the rectangle, as described in step 2, and unpick some of the stitches afterwards. The choice is yours.) Now attach a layer of lightweight fabric to the underside of the wadding. This can be the same as the fabric you have been using, or any other lightweight fabric. It doesn't matter which you use as it is not going to show, but simply provide a surface onto which the underside of the stitching will be attached. In this way the upper side of the flap may be decorated with all sorts of machine-stitching and the untidy underside can be hidden afterwards by sewing back into place the original underside of the flap, which was previously left unstitched 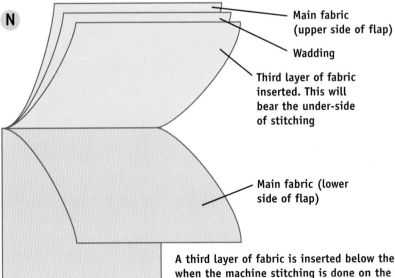.

Main fabric (upper side of flap)

Wadding

Third layer of fabric inserted. This will bear the under-side of stitching

Main fabric (lower side of flap)

A third layer of fabric is inserted below the wadding layer so that when the machine stitching is done on the top of the flap the untidy threads below will be visible on this third layer of fabric. The main fabric which will form the underside of the flap can then be folded back up and sewn in place to conceal the untidy stitching.

Special Effects

This chapter explores the various techniques of manipulating fabric to create extra texture or colour. These include shirring, ruching, ribbon weaving, pleating, embossing, slashed layers, cut-work and dyeing. They can be achieved simply and without specialist equipment, enabling you to transform a plain piece of fabric into something more artistic.

Shirring

For this process, fabric is gathered into folds by means of a special elastic (called shirring elastic), which is wound onto the bobbin in exactly the same way as ordinary cotton. As a line is sewn, the fabric is gathered because the shirring elastic is under tension, producing an effect similar to smocking, but without the fixed pleats characteristic of smocking. By sewing lots of equidistant parallel lines the fabric becomes gathered, creating a smocking effect. Sewing lines in just one direction creates a 'single-shirred' effect, with the fabric gathered in one direction only. For a 'double-shirred' effect, with the fabric gathered in both directions, you must sew a second set of parallel lines perpendicular to the first set. In this way you effectively produce a piece of elasticated fabric which will stretch in all directions.

Shirring is an easy technique, but it is important to bear in mind the following points:

- Because the shirred fabric is gathered, you end up with a piece of fabric which is much smaller than it was before you started, so you must allow for this when planning to make any item from shirred material. It is almost impossible to calculate exactly how much material you will need, so it is strongly recommended that you experiment with a trial piece of the same fabric before you start, measuring the dimensions before and after you have shirred. This will give you a rough idea of how much fabric you need to start with.

- The distance between the sewn parallel lines will determine the extent to which the fabric shrinks in size – the closer the lines, the more it will shrink, because closer lines produce tighter gathers.

- Generally speaking, the finer the fabric, the closer together you will want to sew your lines, and vice versa.

- Use a fairly long stitch (see Tip on facing page). Again, trial and error will help you determine what is most appropriate.

Materials

- Your chosen fabric (here, velvet was used)
- Machine cotton
- Shirring elastic
- Fusible interfacing

Tip

If you need to unpick any stitches, it is easier if you have used a slightly longer stitch.

Instructions

1 Decide on the distance you want between each parallel line of sewing. To determine this it is best to experiment first with different widths of lines to see which effect you like the most. Wind shirring elastic onto the sewing machine bobbin and use ordinary machine sewing cotton for the top thread. Then, starting near the edge of your fabric, sew a long line parallel to the edge of the fabric **A**.

2 Continue to the end of the fabric and, leaving a gap of approximately 3/8 in (1 cm), turn through 90 degrees and sew for the distance you want between each line. Here, because velvet has been used, there is a wide distance between the parallel lines – approximately 2 in (5 cm). You will notice that as you sew, the fabric begins to gather behind the needle. This effect is visible in photo **A**.

3 Turn through 90 degrees in the same direction and sew another long line parallel to the first until you reach the end of the fabric, close to where you started. Try to get the lines as straight and parallel as you can, as this will ensure a neat, even effect. If you think you may have difficulty with this, draw the lines on the fabric first with a temporary marker pen, to act as a guide. As you begin to sew this second line you will notice that the fabric has already started to gather. It is important to stretch the fabric out flat in front of you as you sew, in order to create an even tension in your work. (As you progress you will notice the fabric becoming more tightly gathered.)

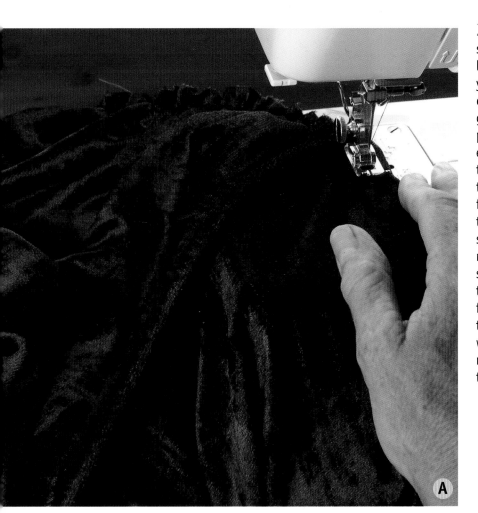

A

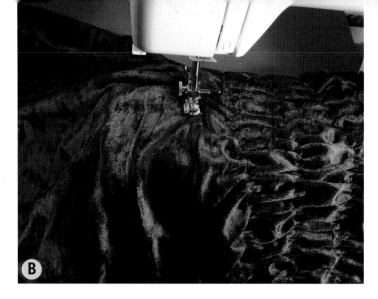

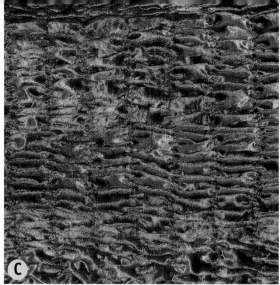

4 Turn through 180 degrees again and sew a third line parallel to the first two. Continue to sew in parallel lines **B** until the entire width of the fabric has been used. Photo **C** shows the single-shirred effect which is created after all the parallel lines have been sewn in one direction. This elasticates the fabric widthways. If you wish to achieve a 'double-shirred' effect, continue with the following steps.

5 Turn the whole fabric through 90 degrees and repeat the entire process, except that this time you will be sewing parallel lines which are perpendicular to the first ones. It is important to continue to stretch the fabric out flat, with your hands in front of the needle as you sew – this is rather more difficult when you are sewing the second set of lines, as the fabric has a tendency to contract in both directions **D**.

6 Continue in this way until the entire fabric has been sewn in both directions. You have now created fabric which is elasticated in all directions. Photo **E** illustrates the 'double-shirred' effect. As mentioned previously, if you use a finer fabric you will need to sew the lines closer together.

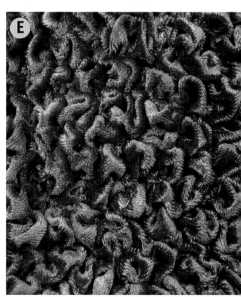

Photo **F** illustrates some silk being shirred. Here the distance between the parallel lines was only 3/8 in (1 cm).

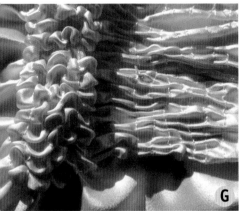

Photo **G** shows the second set of parallel lines sewn. You can clearly see the difference in appearance between the 'single-shirred' and 'double-shirred' effects.

Instead of sewing in straight lines you can also sew in a random 'free-style' fashion to produce a lovely fluid effect **H**.

When you have completed your shirred fabric, you may want to iron some fusible interfacing onto the wrong side, to keep the fabric in the correct shape ready for when you want to use it. Before ironing the interfacing onto the back of the fabric, it is a good idea to place the fabric face down onto a piece of scrap fabric and pin it in place. Whether or not you decide to use interfacing will depend on the purpose for which the fabric is to be used. If you were to use it for a garment, you probably wouldn't want to do this. When using it for bags, however, it is a good idea to use this technique, as it helps to give some rigidity to the fabric and hold it in the right shape.

Ruching

This method of gathering fabric is completely different from the previous one, as it produces a more 'random' effect. This technique involves two layers of fabric: a base layer and a top layer, which is ruched.

Materials

- A piece of fabric that is to form your base layer. This will be the size and shape that you wish your finished article to be, and can either be of the same fabric you are going to use for the ruching or any scrap material, since it will not show
- A piece of fabric for the ruching. Try to use a fabric which reflects the light well, so as to enhance the ruching texture, such as silk, satin, organza or velvet. This piece of fabric needs to be approximately twice the size of your base fabric
- Machine sewing thread
- Strong thread for the running stitches

Note: *The size of your ruching fabric is not critical. If you wish to economize you can use significantly less than double the size. You need to bear in mind, however, that the larger the top fabric in relation to the base layer, the more tightly crinkled the finished effect will be. It is worth experimenting first with some scrap material of a similar weight, to see which effect you like and how much fabric you will need.*

Instructions

1 Cut out your base layer. Here a 6 in (15 cm) diameter circle of plain peach-coloured polyester fabric has been used. Now cut out the fabric that is to be ruched – in this example a 12 in (30 cm) piece of blue polyester **A**.

2 Take the piece of fabric to be ruched and sew a running stitch all around the edge using strong thread **B**. Draw this up so that its circumference fits exactly over that of the base layer. Pin and tack in place onto the base layer.

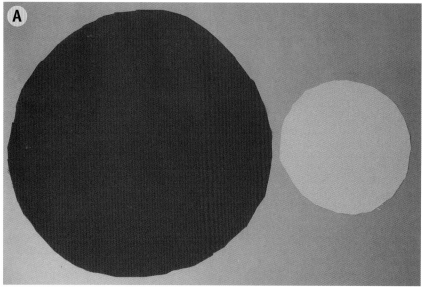

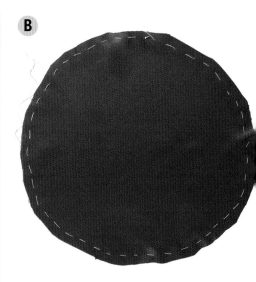

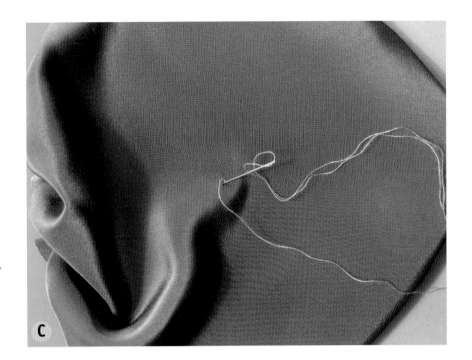

3 Machine-stitch all the way around the edge and remove the tacking stitches and the running-stitch thread. You will now find that the top layer of fabric forms a sort of large, folded 'bubble' over the base layer.

4 Using thread of the same colour as your top fabric, make a tiny stitch roughly in the centre of the 'bubble' and secure it to the base layer **C**. Make several more stitches (roughly equally spaced) around the first stitch, each time securing the top layer to the base layer **D**.

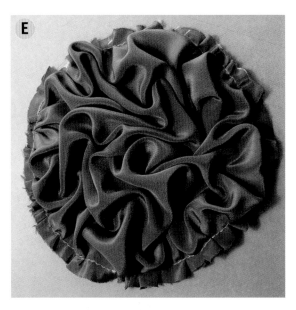

5 Continue in this way, making many more small stitches, anchoring the top layer to the base layer, trying to keep the stitches evenly placed. As you continue the fabric will gradually become more tightly wrinkled **E** **F**. The point at which you stop will depend on how tightly ruched you wish your fabric to be, and the type of effect you are aiming for. Photo **G** shows the back of the fabric, illustrating the random nature of the stitching.

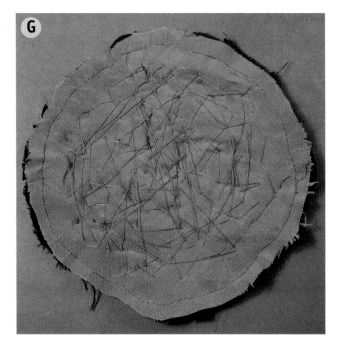

When you have achieved the desired effect, your fabric is ready to be used – for example in the creation of a bag. Remember that you will not want the base layer of fabric to show, so you will need to cover it either with some suitable lining material or with the same fabric that you used for the ruching. Whichever you use will be determined by the design of the article you are making. Similarly, the raw edges will either need to be bound or incorporated into other material by an alternative method. The 'Shimmering Mist' project (see page 41), illustrates the making of a bag using ruched organza.

Ribbon weaving

Ribbon weaving is a technique that allows you to produce a piece of fabric with a latticework of woven ribbon. Depending on the number of colours used and the varying widths of the ribbons, a wide assortment of different patterns and designs can be created. In the example illustrated overleaf, ribbons of four different colours were used, all the same width, approximately 5/8 in (1.5cm).

Materials

- Ribbon, of your chosen colours and widths
- Backing fabric, to which the ribbon will be fused
- Fusible interfacing
- Machine cotton

Instructions

1 First select your backing fabric. The type of fabric you choose will very much depend upon the use to which you will eventually put your ribbon-weave fabric. If both sides of the fabric are to be seen you will want an attractive backing fabric that will complement your ribbons. If the backing fabric is not going to be visible in the finished item, you can use a piece of scrap material.

2 Cut your backing fabric to the desired shape and size. (This should be the same as you wish your finished ribbon-weave fabric to be.)

3 Cut out a piece of fusible interfacing of the same size and shape and iron it to the backing fabric **A** then peel off the backing paper.

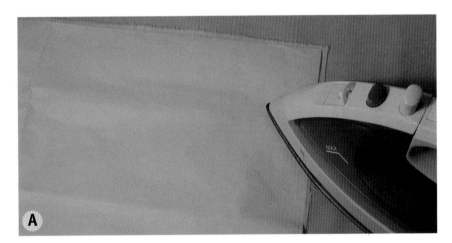

4 Place the backing fabric on a board with the fusible interfacing on the upper side.

5 Cut your ribbon into the required lengths. You need one set of ribbons that are as long as the length of your backing fabric, and some that are the same length as the width of the backing fabric. You will need to calculate how many of each length you will need.

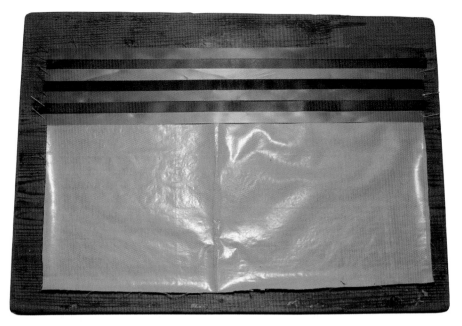

6 Decide how you are going to arrange your ribbons. This will depend on the colours and relative widths you have chosen. It is worth experimenting in order to achieve different patterns.

7 Pin your ribbon sections side by side along the length of the backing fabric, so that they are resting on top of the fusible interfacing **B**. As you do so, make sure the ribbons are straight and pulled taut. Try to avoid any gaps. Continue to do this until all the backing fabric is covered with adjacent rows of ribbon.

B

Note: *Some ribbon is the same on both sides, but others have a noticeable 'right' side and 'wrong' side. If any of your ribbon is not the same on both sides, make sure that you pin it 'right' side up on the backing fabric.*

8 Now cut your shorter set of ribbon sections. Taking one piece at a time, carefully weave them in and out of the previous lines of ribbon **C**. As before, pin each piece of ribbon to the board at both ends to secure it. Continue until the weaving is complete.

9 Carefully cover the fabric with a damp cloth, taking care not to disturb any of the ribbon, then iron the middle section. The fusible interfacing will thus anchor the ribbons to the backing fabric. Gently remove the pins all around the edge and iron the remainder of the fabric. The ribbons should now be firmly bonded to the backing fabric. To safely secure all the ribbon ends, machine-stitch all the way around the edge, approximately 1/4in (0.5cm) from the edge.

10 Optional: If you wish, you can neatly top-stitch each length of ribbon. This makes the ribbon doubly secure and, if done neatly, can create a decorative effect.

C

Embossing

This technique creates a design in relief from the background. It is fairly time-consuming but the finished effect is worth the time and effort. The procedure uses up a great deal of machine thread, so make sure you have plenty before you start.

Note: *Your sewing machine must be capable of having the feed-dogs lowered or, alternatively, have a plate that covers the feed-dogs.*

Materials

- Plenty of machine embroidery thread (preferably a fairly decorative thread, since this will form the background stitching to your design)
- A piece of fabric, ideally such as velvet, satin, silk, or any other material that will catch the light and emphasize the relief
- A piece of wadding the same size as your chosen fabric
- A piece of plain scrap fabric for the backing, again of the same size
- Lining material, if the back of the finished fabric is going to show

Instructions

1 Attach the free-embroidery foot to your sewing machine and lower or cover the feed-dogs.

2 Choose a design, preferably one that is fairly simple, such as Ⓐ, and transfer it onto the piece of scrap backing fabric.

Ⓐ

3 Take your top fabric, wadding and backing fabric **B** and place them one on top of the other with the wadding in the middle and the backing fabric with the design on positioned on top. Pin all three in place **C** then tack in position and remove the pin.

4 With the design on the backing fabric facing uppermost, attach the embroidery hoop to expose a section of your design. Place this under the free-embroidery foot on the sewing machine.

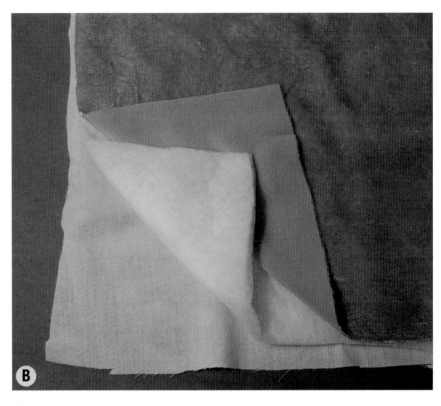

5 Sew all the way round the edge of your design. (You will need to reposition the embroidery hoop at intervals.)

Note: *If your backing fabric is fairly stiff, you may find that you don't need to use an embroidery hoop. It is a good idea to try it first and see. If you don't use a hoop, make sure you sew the outline of your design working from the centre outwards. This will help to prevent the fabric from puckering.*

6 When you have sewn along the outline of the design you need to fill in the background gaps with free-style machine embroidery .

7 Continue in this way until all the background has been filled with stitching. How 'dense' you make the free-style background stitching is up to you. The more you sew the denser it becomes, but it also takes longer and uses more cotton, so it is a good idea, when you start, to create a low- or medium-density all over. Then, if you wish, you can continue with your stitching to increase its density. The most important thing is to keep the density even all over; otherwise it be patchy. Photo **E** shows the finished piece. Note how the design stands out in relief against the sewn background, to create an embossed appearance.

8 Optional: If your piece of embossed fabric is to be used in a project where the back of the fabric will show, sew on some lining material to cover it.

Mexican pleats

Mexican pleats are a series of parallel-stitched pleats, which are then folded backwards and forwards and the folds stitched in place. Like the previous techniques described, this procedure reduces the overall size of the fabric, so it is advisable to practise first on a similar piece of fabric, using the same size and number of pleats, and measure the fabric before and after, in order to discover the amount by which the fabric is reduced in size. It is worth noting that the fabric will only be reduced in length, not width.

The amount by which the length is reduced will depend on the number and size of pleats and the spacing between them. You can roughly calculate the final length of the fabric by multiplying the width of each pleat by the number of pleats and subtracting this from the initial length. This will give the final length.

For example, in the sample detailed here the initial length of the fabric was 28in (71cm). There are ten pleats, each of 1¼in (3.2cm) width. 10 × 1¼in (3.2cm) = 12½in (31.7cm). So if we subtract 12½in (31.7cm) from the initial length of 28in (71cm) that leaves us with 15½in (39.3cm). In actual fact, the final length of the fabric turned out to be slightly less than this, so it is as well to err on the generous side.

As a rough guide, you can use the following equation:
Final length of fabric = initial length − (number of pleats × width of pleats).

Materials

- A piece of fabric that is much longer than you wish the final length to be (for exact length use the calculation above). In this example orange silk was used, with dimensions of 18in (45cm) wide × 28in (70cm) long
- Machine thread

All lines drawn 1¼in apart

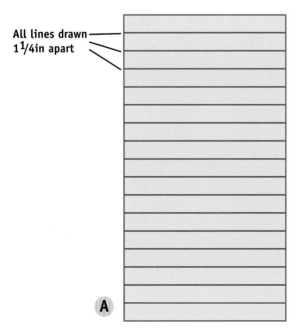

A

Instructions

1 With a temporary marker pen, draw onto the fabric a series of parallel lines across the width A . (The width and number will depend on the size of your fabric and the final effect you wish to achieve, but you will need an even number.) Here, 20 lines were drawn, each positioned 1³/₁₆in (3cm) apart B .

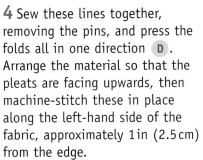

2 With the fabric right side up, starting at one end, place two adjacent lines one on top of the other and pin in place.

3 Repeat with the remaining lines, pinning them together in pairs all down the length of the fabric .

4 Sew these lines together, removing the pins, and press the folds all in one direction D. Arrange the material so that the pleats are facing upwards, then machine-stitch these in place along the left-hand side of the fabric, approximately 1 in (2.5 cm) from the edge.

5 With the pleats folded upwards, and starting at the top left corner of the fabric, fold the top pleat downwards and place a pin 2³/₈ in (6 cm) to the right of the machine-stitched line to secure it. Repeat with the pleat below and continue till all the pleats have been folded downwards and secured with pins E.

6 Tack and remove the pins then stitch the pleats downwards along the line of tacking stitches.

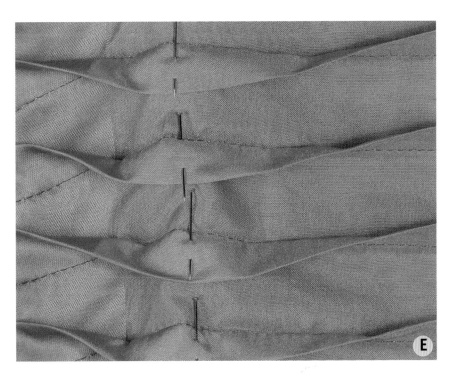

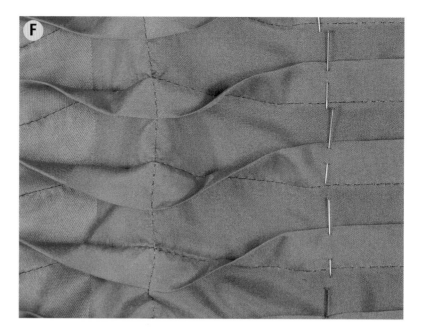

7 Return to the top of the fabric and fold the top pleat back upwards and pin in position 2³/₈ in (6 cm) to the right of the previous line of stitching. Repeat with the pleats below **F**. Pin and tack all the pleats upwards.

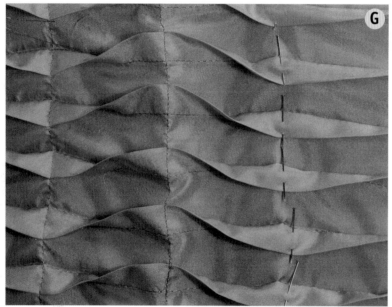

8 Stitch along the tacking lines as before, then return to the top and fold the top pleat downwards again, pinning in place 2³/₈ in (6 cm) to the right of the previous line of stitching. Repeat with the pleats below then tack and machine stitch **G**.

9 Continue in this way until all the pleats have been folded upwards and downwards along the entire width of the fabric **H**. Remove the remains of any tacking thread.

Note: *The final length of the sample fabric shown here was 14¹/₂ in (37 cm), therefore the length had approximately halved by this process.*

Cut-work

Cut-work is a procedure whereby a design is drawn onto fabric, the edges are sewn with satin-stitch, and then the areas inside the lines are cut away. The edges of the fabric are prevented from fraying by the satin-stitch. If a small, intricate design is used this can produce a lacy effect (for example broderie anglaise), or alternatively the fabric can then be placed on top of a different piece of fabric of a contrasting colour so the design is enhanced by the second fabric showing through the cut-away sections.

Materials

- A piece of plain fabric large enough for your chosen project; ideally, the fabric should have a fairly close weave
- Fusible interfacing
- Optional: A second piece of fabric in a contrasting colour

Instructions

1 Find a suitable design – a fairly simple one, with clear lines not too close together. Illustration **A** shows the design used here.

2 Iron fusible interfacing large enough to cover your design and have some overlap, onto the wrong side of your fabric **B**.

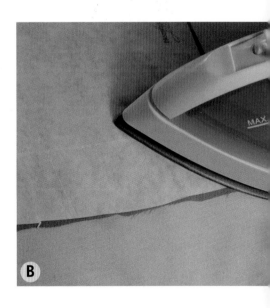

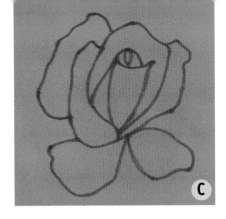
C

3 Transfer your design onto the right side of the fabric C. This can be done with a temporary fabric-marker pen (ideally one with ink that disappears after exposure to the air).

4 Set your sewing machine to the 'satin-stitch' setting and gradually work along all the lines D.

D

E

5 When the lines have been covered with satin-stitch, take a small, sharp pair of scissors and carefully cut out the fabric which occupies the spaces between the sewn lines E. Cut as close as you can to the stitching but be very careful not to cut the thread itself. If you find that the fabric frays you can use anti-fray liquid along the edge.

6 Optional: Place some backing material in a contrasting colour behind the motif. In the example illustrated here, gold fabric has been used F.

F

Slashed layers

Slashing is a technique where several layers of different-coloured fabric are placed one on top of the other and sewn together with a series of fairly close parallel lines. The layers of fabric between each pair of lines is then cut through as far as the bottom layer, which is left intact. Once the layers have been cut, the edges lift very slightly to reveal the different colours. There are several ways to create this effect, but the most commonly used is sometimes referred to as *faux chenille*, and that is the one described here.

There are a few things to you will need to remember when carrying out this particular method:

- The lines of stitching must run diagonally across the weave of the fabric, otherwise it will fray badly and tend to fall apart. This means that you must either cut your fabric 'on the cross' (i.e. diagonally across the weave) and then sew the lines parallel to the sides of the fabric **A**, or you can cut the fabric parallel to the weave but sew your line diagonally across the fabric **B**. Whichever method you choose will depend upon the overall effect you wish to create. It may also depend on how much fabric you happen to have: cutting fabric diagonally across the weave is less economical as more material is wasted at the edges.

- Choose a fabric that does not have a very 'open' weave.

- Use fairly small stitches when sewing your lines so as to secure the layers firmly in place before you start cutting between them.

- Try to use layers of fabric that are contrasting colours, as this will create a more dynamic effect.

- The fabric layers do not need to be all of the same type of fabric, but it is a good idea to use mostly thin fabrics, otherwise it will be more difficult to sew through the layers – silks and satins are ideal.

- The last fabric layer will be the backing, and will not be cut through. Since it will be visible, it shouldn't be scrap fabric but a material that is attractive and enhances the rest of the colour scheme.

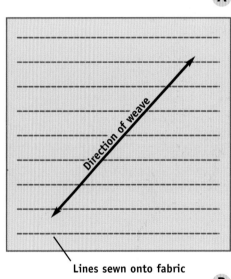

A

Direction of weave

Lines sewn onto fabric

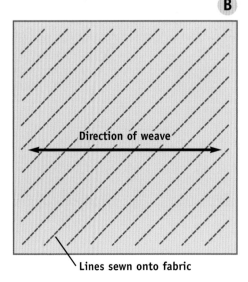

B

Direction of weave

Lines sewn onto fabric

Materials

- Approximately five or six pieces of fabric cut to the required size for your project. In this example squares of 8¼ in (21 cm) were used
- Machine thread

Instructions

1 Cut your layers of fabric to the desired shape and size. In this example each one is cut with the weave running diagonally to the sides.

2 Place the layers on top of one another . Pin them together.

3 Mark a series of parallel lines on the fabric that run diagonally to the weave of the fabric. (In this instance, because the fabrics had been cross-cut, the lines were drawn parallel to the edges.) The lines need to be approximately ³⁄₈ in (1 cm) apart, though this distance is not critical. It is a good idea to experiment with different fabrics and different distances between the lines to decide which effect you prefer.

4 Now machine-stitch along the lines until the entire fabric is covered with evenly spaced parallel lines  .

5 Take a pair of sharp-pointed scissors and carefully cut through the top layers in between each pair of stitch lines. Your cutting lines should be parallel to the stitch lines and mid-way between them. Do not cut through the bottom layer of fabric; this needs to remain intact. Also, do not cut through to the very edge of the fabric – leave a border of at least ²/₃ in (2 cm) all the way round.

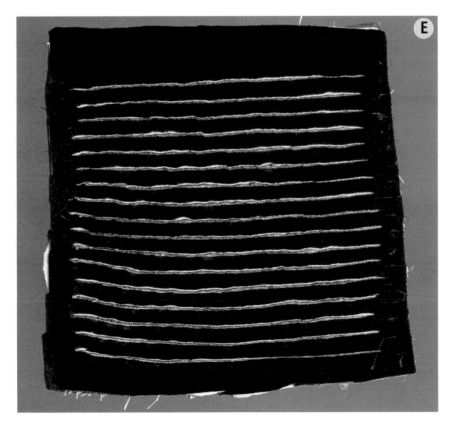

6 After all the cutting has been done you will have the effect of multi-coloured stripes across the fabric as the edges of the cut lines tend to bend upwards slightly. The extreme edges will tend to fray very slightly, creating a rather 'fluffy' texture. Photo E shows the finished effect.

Silk painting

Silk painting, although challenging, offers a wonderful array of different techniques for producing some stunning effects with rich, vibrant hues. It has a long history, especially in the Far East. It is a vast subject and worthy of a book in its own right, so what is offered in these pages is only a brief guide to the art form.

Silk

You can either buy real silk, which tends to be expensive, or synthetic silk, which is a lot cheaper. Both will work well with fabric dyes and paints, but to obtain truly rich and vibrant colours you need to use real silk.

Silk is sold in different weights, and this determines the thickness of the fabric (and the price), so when you buy silk it is worth making sure you know how thick it is. It is easy to buy a relatively cheap length and then arrive home to find it is too thin for your purposes.

The fabric must be thoroughly washed before applying paints or dyes in order to remove any finishing products put on by the manufacturers. This can make a big difference to the way in which the dye is taken up by the fabric and failure to wash the fabric may result in weaker colours. After washing, the fabric should be thoroughly dried and ironed.

Paints and dyes

There is a wide range of silk paints and dyes available on the market and they tend to differ in terms of method of application, method of fixing and their opacity. It is worth buying a small selection of different brands and experimenting because some produce much better results than others. You also need to decide what sort of silk painting or dyeing you want to do. Do you want to immerse the whole fabric in a dye bath to change the colour completely, or do you want to paint designs on with a paintbrush? Some silk dyes and paints are produced primarily for one method or the other. Here we will focus on painting designs rather than immersing the fabric in a dye bath.

Another consideration is the type of dye and the type of fabric. Some dyes are produced specifically for cellulose fibres, such as cotton, linen and viscose, while others are produced for fibres such as wool and nylon. Some will dye both.

For painting designs onto silk you have a choice of either paints or dyes. Generally speaking, paints tend to be slightly more opaque than dyes, although there is some overlap. My personal preference is for transparent rather than opaque pigments, since they allow the lustre of the silk to shine through without losing any of the vibrancy of the colours. Paints also tend to be more viscose, so they don't travel across the fibres as readily, but tend to remain where they have been painted, This means that designs can be painted on without the need for any 'resist' methods (see page 140).

Another consideration is the method of fixing. Dyes need to be fixed in some way so that they don't wash out or fade after long exposure to sunlight. Some dyes have a fixative combined with them, which works simply by drying and exposure to the air, so no further procedure needs to be performed after application. More commonly, many dyes have to be fixed by heat – either by ironing or exposure to heat in some other way, for example by placing in an oven or microwave. Other dyes must have a fixing agent added to them. It is worth finding out what method of fixing is required before you buy.

Silk dyes are usually of the same consistency as water, in other words they are very runny (unless a thickening agent is added to increase their viscosity). When applied to silk with a paintbrush they will, therefore, be absorbed quickly by the fabric and will travel outward in all directions through the fibres. This attractive effect can be exploited by merging different colours together, and by the careful addition of more dye to strengthen the hue in certain areas, or by applying water to lighten the tone. Furthermore, by sprinkling on some coarse granules of rock salt, or sea salt, beautiful speckled patterns can be achieved. Very much depends on how much dye is loaded onto the brush, the thickness of the brush and the concentration of the dye. The best way to discover the multitude of different effects is to spend some time playing and experimenting with various brushes, colours and brushstrokes. Photos A and B show two very different examples of how colours can be merged and blended to create interesting effects.

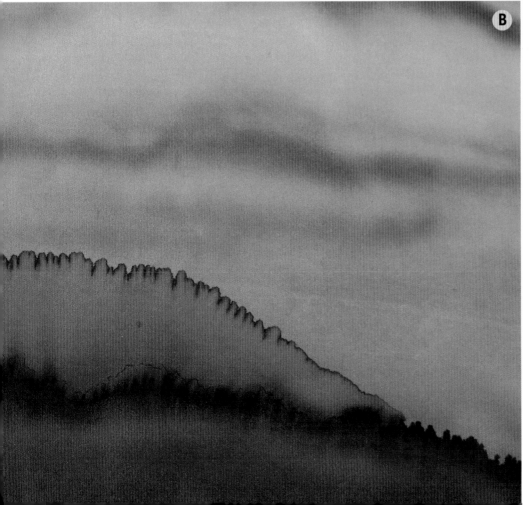

Frame

If you are going to paint a design onto silk that involves outlining techniques, you must pin your silk onto a wooden frame before you start. If you are using a small piece of silk then you can stretch it across an embroidery hoop, but for larger pieces an adjustable wooden frame is ideal or, failing that, an old picture frame. The important thing is to ensure that the silk is pulled tightly and evenly across the frame.

Resist methods

When painting a design onto silk, a common method is to draw the outlines with a 'resist'. This is any compound that will resist the dye and stop it from travelling along the fabric's fibres. Most of us, in our childhood, have tried 'wax resist' techniques by rubbing wax crayons across paper, painting watercolour paint on top, then noticing how the wax resists the flow of the paint. This is the same principle.

The process known as batik, which is a very common method of painting on silk and cotton in South East Asia, involves the application of hot, melted wax onto the fabric in order to delineate the outlines of the design. The hot wax is applied using a tool called a djanting (also known as tjanting or canting). This usually consists of a short length of bamboo, or other wood, about 7in (18cm) in length, at the end of which is attached a small metal cup with a fine spout Ⓒ. The cup is filled with hot wax, which is then applied to the cloth by running the spout across it and 'drawing' the lines of the design on with the hot wax. After the wax is dry, dyes are painted onto the fabric between the lines. Eventually the fabric is washed in very hot water to remove the wax. The temperature of the wax when it is applied is critical: too hot and it will be absorbed too readily into the fabric and will 'pool' out into thicker lines, too cool and it will sit on the surface of the fabric rather than being absorbed by the fibres, resulting in the dye 'bleeding' through the lines. Thus, the traditional method of batik requires skill, and a container of hot wax, which can be very messy.

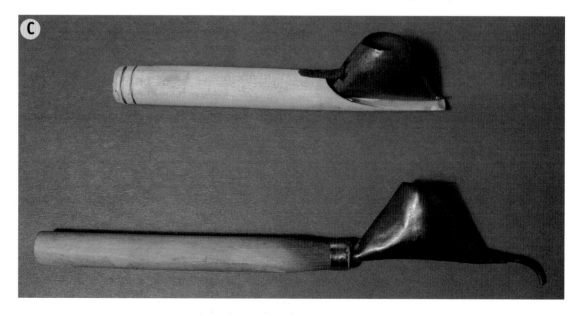

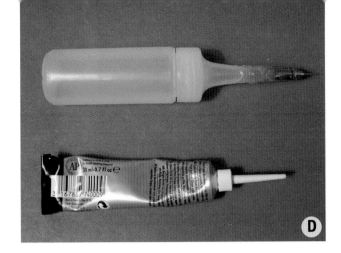

Fortunately, there is an alternative to hot wax, which achieves the same effect but more easily and less messily. This is a product called gutta, which is available in most craft stores. It is sold in squeezable plastic bottles with detachable fine metal spouts, or in squeezable tubes D . By squeezing lines of gutta onto the fabric, the outline of the design can be delineated in exactly the same way as with hot wax. Photo E shows gutta being applied from a tube. The gutta is absorbed into the fabric and resists the flow of the dye. Traditionally it is colourless, but it can also be bought in black, grey, gold and silver for some interesting effects. Some brands of gutta are designed to wash out after the dyeing process, leaving white lines. Other forms stay in after washing. Whichever type you use, it is recommended that you spend some time practising first on a piece of scrap material, as even with easy-to-apply gutta that comes in tubes, it still requires quite a knack (and a steady hand) to get it right. In photo F a simple effect has been achieved by applying dye to silk in between lines of gutta, which have resisted the flow of the dye.

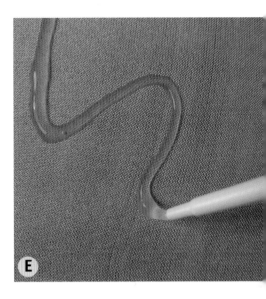

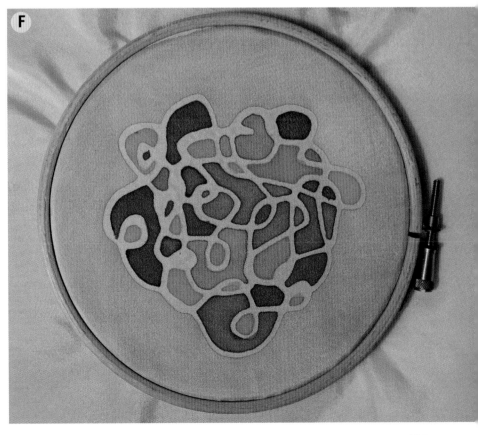

Creating Motifs

A motif, in the context of this book, can be any design, symbol or pattern that is created to embellish a piece of work. There is no limit to the variety of motifs that can be made; the themes or designs depend very much on the type of item for which they are intended. In this book most of the motifs are designs inspired by nature, such as flowers, insects, leaves and fruit. This chapter, continues this theme and shows how inspiration from nature can be translated into decorative motifs.

There are many ways in which motifs can be constructed. For example, you can create two-dimensional motifs, which can be sewn or heat-bonded onto a flat surface. Alternatively, you can create three-dimensional motifs, which can be sewn onto a surface and then protrude. Then there are those that are a mixture of the two.

This chapter describes a range of motif designs and methods of construction, all varying in complexity. Remember, though, there are no rules: the methods described here are suggestions, not definitive procedures.

Motif 1: A slice of fruit

This is a two-dimensional 'flat' motif representing a slice of lemon. The template is on page 156. Other fruit motifs, such as those needed for Tutti Frutti on page 19, can be made in the same way.

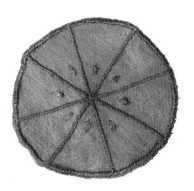

Materials

- A piece of yellow chiffon measuring approximately 8 × 4in (20 × 10 cm)
- Angelina fibres
- Gold metallic thread
- A temporary marker pen

Instructions

1 Tease out the Angelina fibres so they are evenly distributed over an area measuring roughly 4 in (10 cm) square. Place them between two sheets of baking parchment and iron them with a hot iron. (Take care not to let any of the Angelina fibres touch the bottom of the iron, as they would melt onto it.) This will fuse the fibres into a fairly stiff, flat, shimmering sheet. The sheet should be roughly the same shape and size as the folded chiffon **A**.

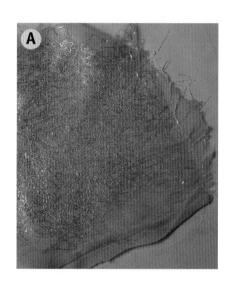

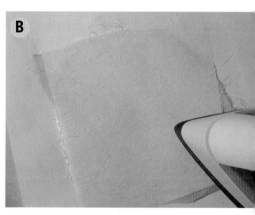

2 Place the Angelina sheet inside the folded chiffon to create a 'chiffon sandwich'. Alternatively, instead of ironing the Angelina fibres first, you can place them directly inside the folded chiffon and iron them both at the same time. (If you choose this method, make sure that you place a piece of paper or baking parchment over the top so that nothing melts onto the bottom of your iron) **B**.

3 Using a temporary marker pen, draw a design of a lemon slice, indicating the segments **C**.

4 Using a sewing machine that is set to 'satin-stitch', sew along the lines D.

Note: *When machine-stitching motifs, regardless of which type of stitch you are using, it is necessary to sew onto fabric that is fairly stiff, otherwise the fabric will tend to pucker and its shape will become distorted. On its own, chiffon would not normally be stiff enough, but the addition of the Angelina fibres provides extra stiffness as well as adding a shimmering effect. Ironing on fusible interfacing would have the same effect of stiffening the fabric, thus making motifs easy to sew as well as enabling them to be attached through heat-bonding. When making a motif from a piece of thin fabric that has not been artificially stiffened, it will be necessary to stretch the fabric across an embroidery hoop. The hoop is then slid under the machine foot and sewing can continue as normal, because the fabric is being stretched out and will therefore hold its shape.*

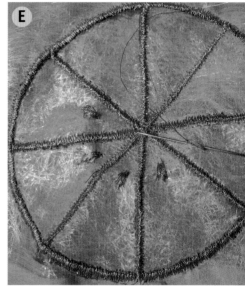

5 When you have sewn all the lines, hand-stitch the 'pips' in between the segments E.

6 Carefully cut around the outside edge of the satin-stitch. It is important to get as close as you can to the stitching without actually cutting any of it F.

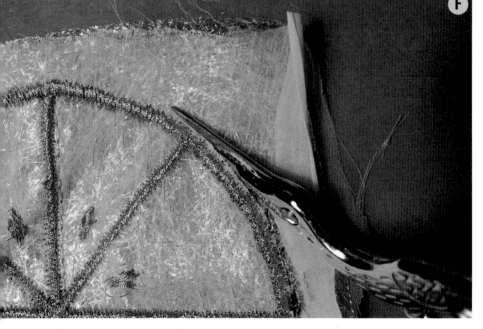

Motif 2: A simple leaf

This design is what one might call a 'generic leaf' since it is not intended to represent any particular type. It is one of the easiest motifs to make. The method described here involves the use of a specialized soldering iron, which has a pointed tip, to cut and fuse the edges of the fabric and thus prevent fraying. Because of this, it is important you use a fabric made from synthetic fibres (for more details, see page 101). A template for this leaf is on page 156.

Materials

- A piece of green synthetic felt (sometimes called counin felt) measuring approximately 3 in (8 cm) square
- One or two pieces of synthetic organza also measuring approximately 3 in (8 cm) square
- Metallic thread
- A stiff, heat-resistant template of some kind around which to 'draw' the shape with the soldering iron. I used a tin lid, approximately 3 in (8 cm) in diameter

Note: *It is important to use a sheet of glass to work on while soldering; this will provide a firm, flat surface that will not become damaged by the tip of the soldering iron.*

Instructions

1 Cut out your squares of felt and organza to the dimensions given above **A**.

2 Position your one piece of organza either on top of the square of felt or place your felt between your two pieces of organza to create a 'sandwich'.

Note: *It doesn't really matter whether you use one piece of organza or two, as in either case the heat from the soldering iron will fuse the felt and organza together around the edges. The only difference is that if you make a 'sandwich' using two pieces of organza, then you will have the organza on both the top and the bottom surfaces. This is a matter of personal preference that depends on how you wish to use the motif.*

3 Place the fabric layers onto a piece of glass, then put your template on the fabric and 'draw' round one side of it with the hot soldering iron, as shown in photo B . The soldering iron will simultaneously cut out the shape and fuse the fabric layers together at the edges.

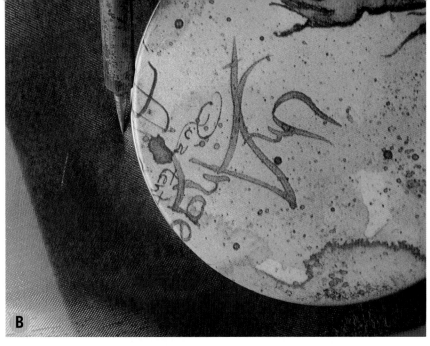

B

C

D

4 Now move the template so that it cuts an identical curve in the opposite direction, cutting across the first one. This will create the leaf shape C .

5 Using metallic thread machine-stitch all around the edge with satin-stitch and then with a straight stitch sew in the lines of the veins D .

Motif 3: A lacy leaf

Sometimes you may wish to produce a very delicate motif with a lacy effect, consisting of stitching without fabric. With an ordinary sewing machine, this would be extremely difficult to achieve, but now there are all sorts of different water-soluble fabrics that can be used to obtain this effect (see page 99). The stitching is first done on the water-soluble fabric. When complete, the whole piece is immersed in water. The fabric dissolves away instantly and you are left with just the stitching. The example shown here was inspired by a nasturtium leaf (see template on page 157).

Materials

- Enough water-soluble fabric to be attached to the hoop
- Two different types of green machine cotton – one satin and one metallic

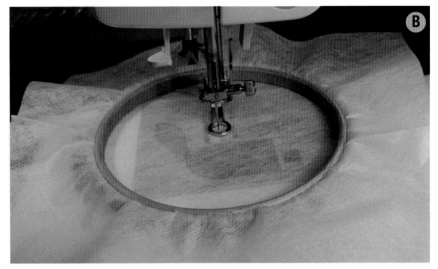

(A)

(B)

Instructions

1 Draw your design onto water-soluble fabric or, as it is slightly transparent, trace onto it if you prefer (A). It is important to make sure that your motif will 'hold together' after the fabric has dissolved away, so choose a design that is fairly compact, with sewing lines that link up with each other.

2 Set up your sewing machine for free-style embroidery. This will normally involve lowering or covering the feed-dogs and attaching a free-style embroidery foot. (Refer to your sewing-machine instruction book.)

3 Place the water-soluble fabric in the embroidery hoop and slide this under the sewing foot (B).

Note: *It is not essential to use an embroidery hoop – it depends on the type of water-soluble fabric you are using and how stiff it is. If it is fairly stiff you may be able to manage without, but you will need to keep the fabric stretched quite taut between your fingers and work from the centre outwards.*

(C)

4 Using free-style embroidery, sew over the lines drawn onto the water-soluble fabric. Once this is done you can sew in additional lines if you wish. Here, two types of machine cotton were used: one satin and one metallic (C).

5 Place the fabric in water (following the instructions for that particular brand). The fabric will dissolve instantly, leaving the thread behind. There may be a slight reduction in the overall size of the motif after the fabric has dissolved. Photo (D) shows the finished motif after the fabric has disappeared. You can then place the motif on a different piece of fabric if you wish, so that the new fabric shows through the gaps (E).

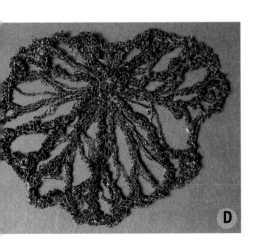

(D)

(E)

Motif 4: A maple leaf

The following method of creating a motif is extremely simple and versatile, and can be adopted for a whole range of motifs, although here a maple leaf was the inspiration. It involves using a product commercially sold as Stitch 'n' Tear which is designed as a backing material for fabric to give it the required 'stiffness' for decorative embroidery. Although it is reasonably strong, it can be easily torn away from the main fabric and its stitching. There are three maple leaf templates to choose from on page 158.

Materials

- A piece of green fabric, such as silk, chiffon, organza, or satin. In this example a piece of hand-dyed silk was used. It needs to be approximately 4 in (10 cm) square
- A piece of Stitch 'n' Tear of the same dimensions
- Metallic machine thread
- Optional: Dimensional fabric paint

Instructions

1 Draw your design onto the chosen fabric (in this example, silk) **A** .

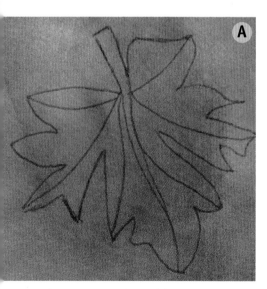

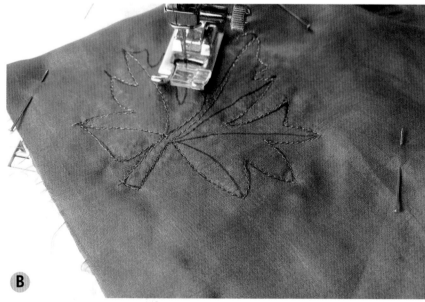

2 Pin the fabric to the Stitch 'n' Tear to hold it in place. Machine-stitch around the edge of the motif first, with a straight stitch to hold the two fabrics in position and prevent distortion, then remove the pins **B** .

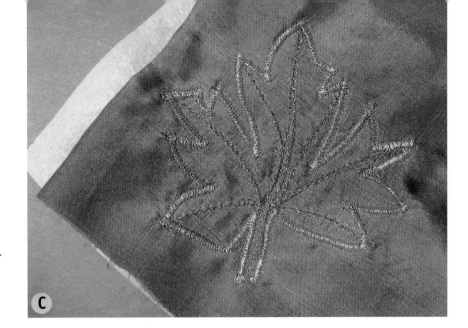

3 Now sew with satin-stitch over all the perimeter lines. The veins can be sewn in with ordinary straight stitch **C**.

4 Remove the fabric from the machine, turn it over to the back, and tear away the Stitch 'n' Tear fabric from the entire motif, leaving just the silk **D**.

5 Optional: You may wish to add some spots of dimensional fabric paint. The type illustrated here is called 'Tulip crystals' and consists of tiny translucent pigments that, when dry, reflect the light and the colour of the fabric on which they are placed **E**.

Note: *Instead of using Stitch 'n' Tear you can use fusible interfacing. Iron it on to the back of the fabric prior to stitching and then remove the backing paper when cool. The adhesive layer provides sufficient stiffness to be able to do machine embroidery without the need for a hoop. The added advantage is that the motif is then ready to be directly heat-bonded to your chosen item.*

Motif 5: Ribbon flower

This motif, representing a generic flower, is one of the easiest to make. So far, the motifs described have been two-dimensional, but this one is three-dimensional and made from wired ribbon. When secured at one end and pulled from the other, the ribbon gathers into pleasing folds.

Materials

- A length of wired ribbon, approximately 24 in (60 cm) long and 2 in (5 cm) wide
- A handful of small beads
- Sewing thread

Instructions

1 Take your ribbon and locate the end of one of the pieces of wire. Either knot it or fold it back on itself tightly to secure the end and prevent it being pulled through.

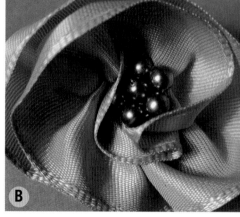

2 Now take the other end of this piece of wire and gently pull it. As you do so, the ribbon will begin to gather into folds **A**. Continue until the entire length of ribbon is gathered. Arrange the folds and secure the free end with a few hand-stitches.

3 Thread together a cluster of small beads and sew these to the centre **B**. Further embellishments can also be added, such as pretty ribbons and feathers.

Motif 6: Organza flowers

To make this motif you need to use a pointed soldering iron, as described on page 101. It is important that your fabric is a synthetic organza, so that the fibres melt and fuse as they are cut. The great advantage to this technique is that because the edges are fused they cannot fray. Like the previous motif, these flowers are also generic and three-dimensional. You will find the templates for them on page 158.

Materials

- Some pieces of organza, preferable different colours
- Sewing thread
- Seed beads

Instructions

1 It is not necessary to draw a design onto the organza for this, or even use a metal template, unless you really want to. All you need to do is to take the hot soldering iron and, holding the fabric flat on a piece of glass – you may find it useful to weight down the edges first – draw some rough five- or six-petalled flower shapes with the tip of the soldering iron. They can be any size you want, depending on the size of motif you wish to make. Photo **A** shows the soldering iron cutting out the shapes. Photo **B** shows three rough flower shapes. Ideally you need about six or seven of the shapes to make one flower.

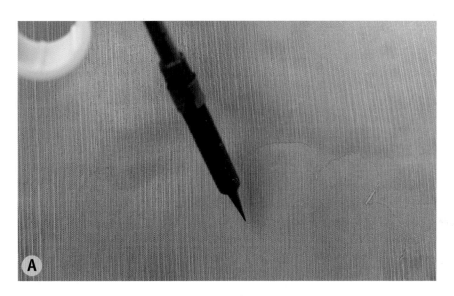

2 Take your flower shapes, lay them one on top of the other then, using the needle and cotton, secure them with a few stitches in the centre **C**.

3 Lastly, sew a cluster of seed beads into the centres **D**.

Motif 7: Fuchsia

There are many different ways in which this motif can be created, but I find this method the most straightforward. The template can be found on page 160.

Materials

- A piece of red satin measuring approximately 4 in (10 cm) square
- A piece of fusible interfacing the same dimensions (alternatively Stitch 'n' Tear backing material could be used)
- A piece of purple satin measuring approximately 6 × 3 in (15 × 8cm)
- Red metallic machine thread
- 5in (12cm) of coloured wire
- Six seed beads
- A small piece of green satin measuring approximately 2 in (5 cm) square

Instructions

1 Prepare the red satin by ironing on some fusible interfacing. This will provide the stiffness you require for the machine embroidery without the need for an embroidery hoop. Alternatively you can use Stitch 'n' Tear but the advantage of the fusible interfacing is that the fabric can then be heat-bonded to your chosen item. At this stage you can either peel the backing paper off or leave it on for extra stiffness while stitching. Here, the paper has been left on.

2 Pin the template onto the satin and draw around the edge with a temporary marker pen **A**.

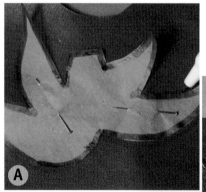

3 Using red metallic machine-thread, sew satin-stitch all around the edges **B**. Photo **C** shows the motif with the outside edges sewn in satin-stitch.

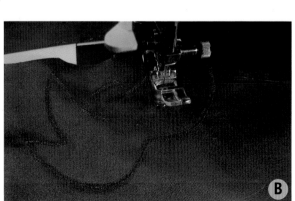

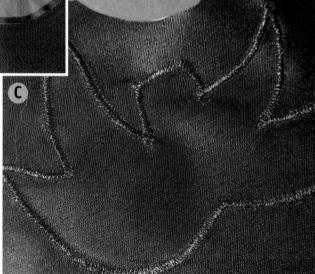

4 Use satin-stitch to fill in the petal lines in the middle of the fabric (indicated by the dotted lines on the template). Then, with fine-pointed scissors, cut around the edge of the stitching as close as you can without cutting any the threads **D**.

5 If you haven't done so at an earlier stage, peel off the backing paper from the fusible interfacing **E**. Here the paper was removed after the initial stitching.

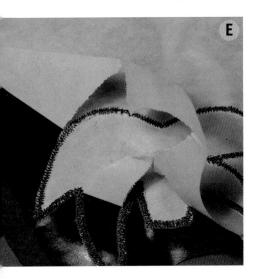

6 Optional: Taking your small piece of green satin, fold it into a rough cone shape and hand-sew it to the top of the petal section to create the base of the stalk **F**. The remainder of the stem can be created from embroidery stitching, ribbon, stuffed ribbon yarn, cord, or any other similar method, depending on the size of your motif and the nature of the item onto which it will be applied.

7 Take your piece of purple satin, fold it in half lengthways and carefully roll and fold it as shown in photo **G**.

8 This purple roll of petals can now be stitched to the underside of the red petal section.

9 Cut your coloured wire into three equal lengths, each approximately 1½ in (4 cm) long and attach one or two seed beads to the ends **H**. Insert these inside the middle of the roll of purple petals **I**. They can be attached either by stitching, or with a dab of 'impact adhesive', or both for extra security.

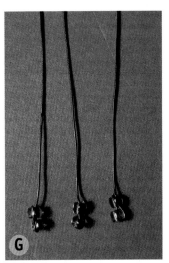

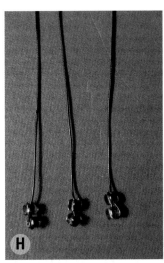

Motif 8: Butterfly

This is the most challenging of all the motifs and it combines a range of techniques. The templates for the various components of the butterfly can be found on page 161.

Materials

- A piece of pink organza approximately 12 in (30 cm) square for the body and lower wings
- A piece of mauve chiffon approximately 13 in (32 cm) square for the upper wings
- A piece of mauve satin approximately 4 in (10 cm) square for the upper wing additions

- Different shades of mauve and purple metallic machine thread
- Silver gutta
- 4 in (10 cm) of coloured wire for the antennae
- Four seed beads for the antennae
- A piece of wadding measuring approximately 6¼ × 5 in (16 × 13 cm) for the lower wing sections

- About 20 small seed beads for the eyes
- A small piece of fusible interfacing approximately 4 × 3 in (10 × 7 cm)
- A temporary marker pen
- A small piece of wadding or cotton wool
- Angelina fibres

Instructions

1 Using the templates for the wing sections on page 161, or your own if you prefer, draw or trace the designs onto paper and cut them out to create your own templates. (You can scale them up or down in size.)

2 Make the body as follows. Take a small piece of pink organza, measuring 8 × 2 in (20 × 5 cm) and a small piece of cotton wool **A**.

3 Fold the organza in half and machine-stitch one long edge and one short edge. Fold right sides out and place the roll of cotton wool or wadding inside. **B**. Fold the raw edges inwards and hand-stitch them securely. You should now have a 'tube' of organza stuffed with cotton wool.

4 Wrap some fairly strong pink metallic cotton tightly at intervals around the tube to delineate sections for the head, thorax and abdomen segments **C**.

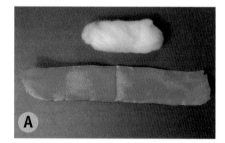

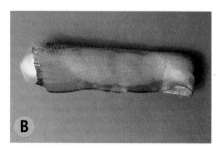

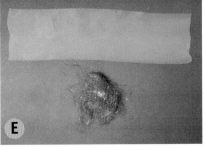

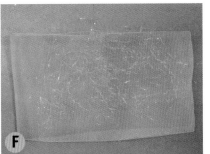

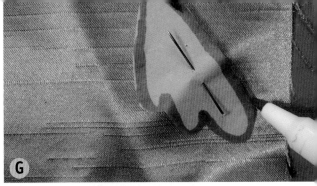

E

F

G

H

D

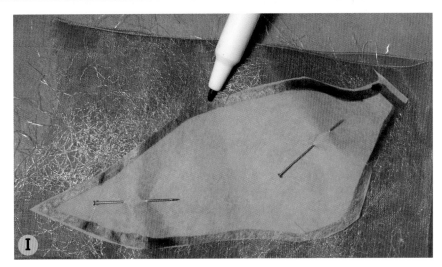

I

5 Cut the coloured wire into two sections, each approximately 2 in (5 cm) long, and attach a couple of seed beads to the ends to represent the antennae. Insert these into the top of the head section and secure with a small dab of impact adhesive.

6 Thread together two small clusters of seed beads for the eyes and sew these to the sides of the head **D**. The body is now complete.

7 Take a length of mauve chiffon approximately 13 × 3 in (32 × 8 cm) and some Angelina fibres **E**. Fold the chiffon in half, with the Angelina fibres on the inside, between the two layers of chiffon. Iron this flat between two sheets of paper to create a 'chiffon sandwich' **F**.

8 Take the upper wing template and, using a temporary marker pen, draw around it onto the piece of chiffon **G**.

9 Remove the template and machine-stitch with satin-stitch all around the edge. The Angelina fibres should provide enough stiffness to sew without the use of a hoop. However, if you don't find this to be the case, you can keep the paper template pinned or tacked onto the chiffon while you sew. After sewing around the edge, cut off the surplus fabric as close as you can to the stitching without actually cutting any of the thread **H**.

10 Draw around the template for the upper wing, onto the piece of mauve satin **I**. Iron some fusible interfacing onto the wrong side of the satin, on the back of the design. This will provide stiffness and enable it to be fused onto the upper wing later **J**.

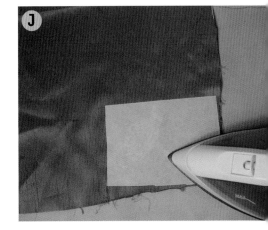

J

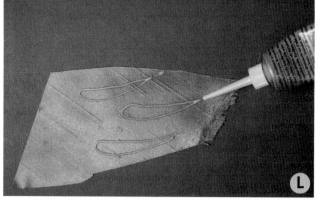

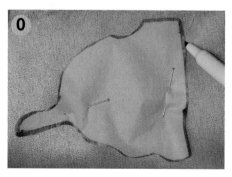

11 Now satin-stitch all around the edge with metallic thread. Using a straight stitch, sew additional decorative lines along the length of the piece K then cut out the shape as before.

12 Onto some remaining satin or organza, delicately draw three elongated teardrop shapes with silver gutta from a tube L (see description of gutta on page 139). When the gutta is thoroughly dry, cut out the shapes.

13 Iron on the addition to the upper wing and then stitch the elongated teardrop shape in place, as shown in photo M. The upper wing is now complete. Repeat steps 7–13 to make the wing on the opposite side. *Make sure you reverse all the shapes.*

14 Now make the lower wing as follows. Take a piece of pink organza approximately 7 × 5in (18 × 12cm). Fold it in half and place a piece of wadding inside to make a 'sandwich' N.

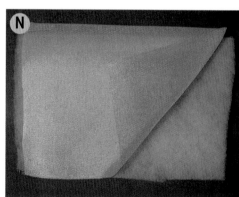

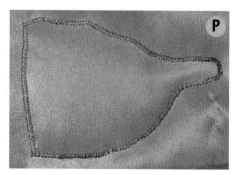

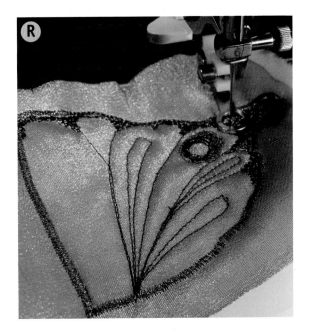

15 With a temporary marker pen, draw around the template for the lower wing, onto the organza 'sandwich' **O**. Then, using metallic machine thread, satin-stitch around the outline **P**.

16 Using a straight stitch on the machine, sew some decorative lines onto the wing with metallic thread, as shown in photo **Q**.

17 Now set up your sewing machine for free-style embroidery and fill-in certain areas with free-style stitching **R** **S**. This completes the lower wing. Repeat steps 14–17 to make the other lower wing, remembering to reverse all the shapes. You should now have in front of you one body, two upper wings and two lower wings.

18 Assemble all the pieces and then sew them together on the underside of the body **T**.

Note: *For some inspirational and highly skilful, anatomically correct designs based on nature, take a look at* The Art of Annemieke Mein. *There you will find some marvellous illustrations of spectacular embroidered representations of insects, birds and other living forms.*

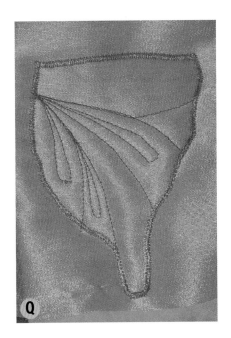

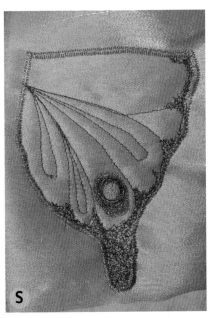

Template 1: A slice of fruit

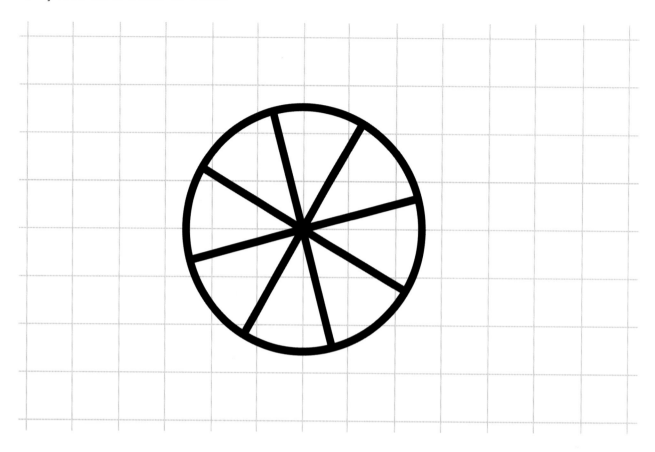

Template 2: A simple leaf

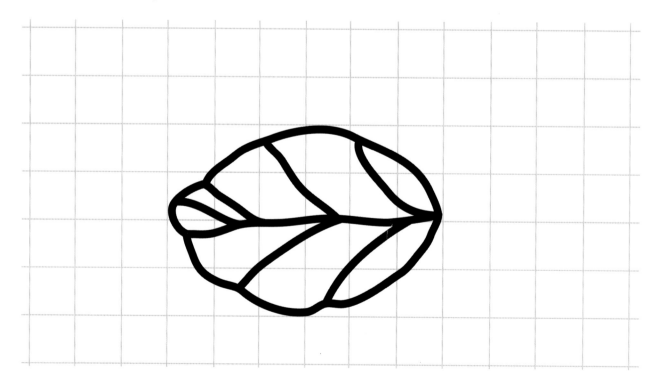

Template 3: A lacy leaf

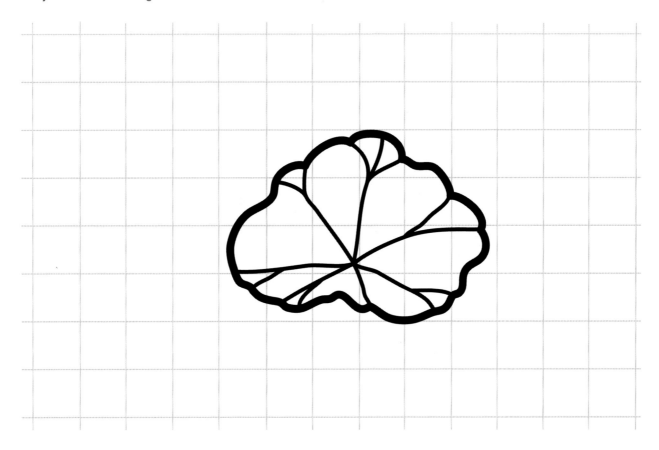

Template 4: Maple leaves

Template 5: Organza flowers

Template 7: Butterfly

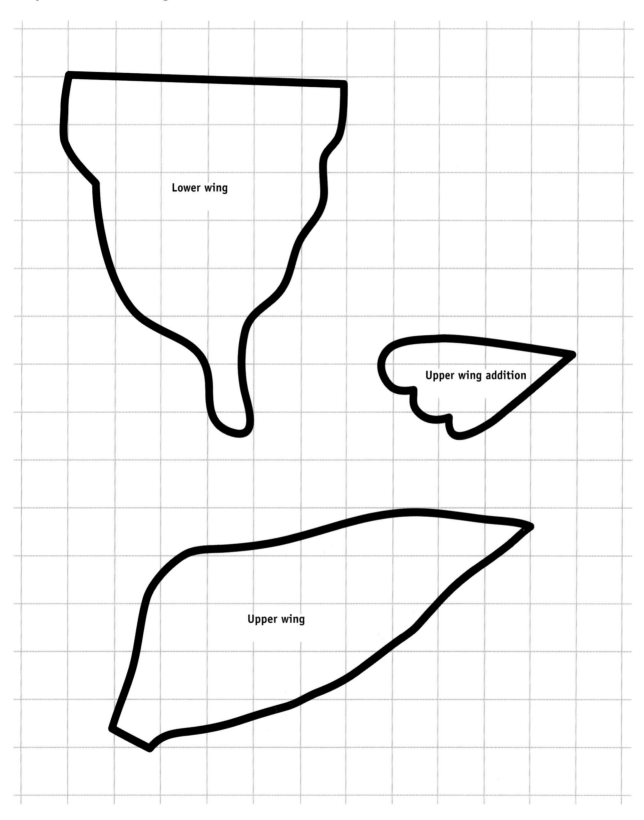

Lower wing

Upper wing addition

Upper wing

Embellishments

There is no limit to the variety of ways in which fabric can be embellished. All manner of things can be sewn on to add decoration. For instance, I have seen seedpods and cinnamon sticks sewn onto bags with ribbon as part of a 'natural' decorative theme. Here, just a few key examples are discussed.

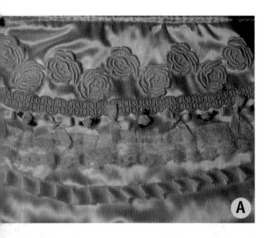

Ribbons and braids

There is an astonishing array of ribbons available today, all differing in colour, width and material. Silk, satin, velvet, organza and cotton – in pastel colours, or dazzling hues, shimmery, gauzy and glittery – the choice is endless. Some ribbon has wire threaded all the way along both edges, which can be pulled to gather the ribbon into ruffles and coils. Braid is also widely available in a huge variety of colours and widths. Both ribbons and braids can be used to good effect to create rich, sumptuous designs. Photo A (Dream Wedding, on page 81) shows an example of a bag decorated this way.

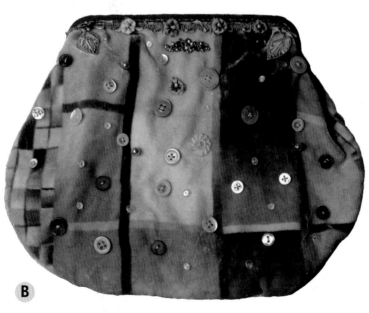

Buttons, sequins, beads, shells & feathers

Bags covered in buttons or sequins are currently very fashionable, especially since, as with ribbons and braids, there is such a wide range available. I have seen some most unusual buttons hand-crafted from polymer clay and ceramic clay. Mother-of-pearl buttons can be very attractive and photo **B** (Granny's Treasure, on page 87) gives an illustration of a bag decorated with these.

Other natural objects, such as shells and feathers, can be sewn onto fabric, too. (With shells it is sometimes necessary to drill a small hole somewhere in order to attach the thread.) Photos **C** and **D** show feathers sewn onto bags for additional decoration.

Because of the huge selection available these days, beads are extremely versatile. There are some beautiful large glass beads (some hand-crafted), which in themselves are a work of art, and one on its own can add a perfect finishing touch to an item. Small clusters of medium-sized beads can create the effect of stamens inside a flower **E** **F**.

Tiny seed beads can be threaded together in patterns or strings to decorate the bottom of a bag in the form of a fringe, see photos G H and I . Alternatively, they can be sewn on in lines to accentuate an existing pattern or form J K . In addition, seed beads can be threaded into three-dimensional forms, such as the 'blackberries' illustrated in photo L .

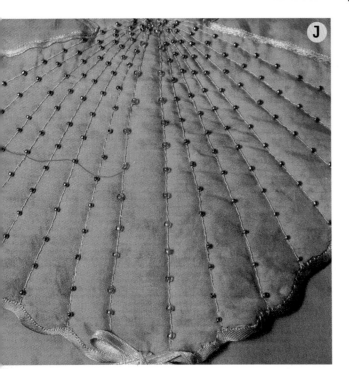

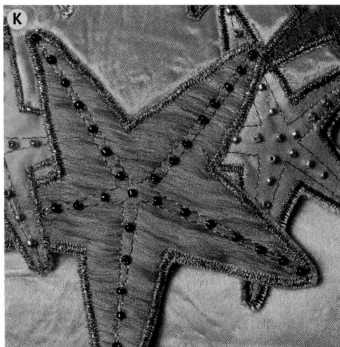

Couched threads

There are a number of ways of creating couched threads, but perhaps the easiest is by setting your sewing machine to a wide zigzag stitch and sewing along either side of a piece of a medium-thickness yarn or thick thread (see diagram **M**). Photo **N** shows thick white woollen yarn being couched with glittery machine cotton. Photo **O** shows the finished yarn after having been couched.

—Machine-sewn zigzag stitch

—Yarn or thick thread

M

Tip

When couching the woollen yarn, it will go between the feed dogs, not over them, and so will not pass under the foot automatically. It is necessary, therefore, to pull the yarn slowly and steadily from behind, so that the needle sews along its length evenly.

N

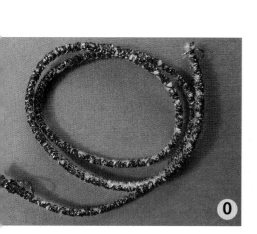

O

After couching, your yarns can then be sewn onto your fabric to create patterns, or hang down from an edge to create a thick fringe. Alternatively, they could be sewn around the edge of an item to form a trim.

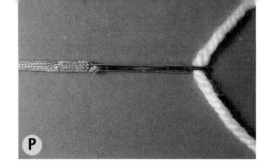

Stuffed ribbon yarn

Ribbon yarn is usually made from a form of viscose, and is used for hand-knitting. It is actually constructed in the shape of a flattened tube, so although it looks just like a flat, tape-like yarn it is actually tubular. Because of this it can be stuffed with thick wool to make it three-dimensional. This is easily and quickly done by threading some thick wool onto a darning needle and passing the needle through the middle of the length of the ribbon yarn P ; you can then cut it off at any length you wish. Photo Q shows the finished yarn coiled and stitched onto fabric. Stuffed ribbon yarn can be used to embellish fabric in the same way as couched threads.

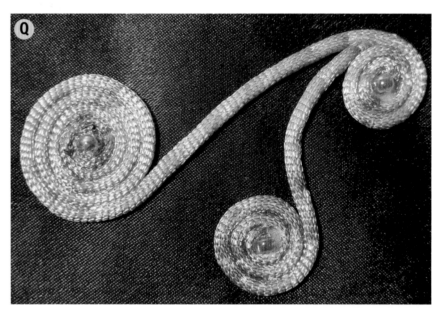

Cord

Cords can also be used to embellish fabric in the same way as couched threads or stuffed ribbon yarn, and it can, if thick enough, be used for bag shoulder straps. Although it is possible to buy cord in a wide variety of colours, patterns and thicknesses, it is fun to make your own. Also, the advantage of doing so is that you can construct it out of any mixture of threads or yarns you wish and can therefore coordinate your cord with your fabric. The method of construction is simple. First you need to decide how thick and how long you want your cord to be. Then decide how many strands you are going to start working with. If you want thick cord it is a good idea to use fairly thick thread or yarn, otherwise it will take ages and you will need a great deal of it.

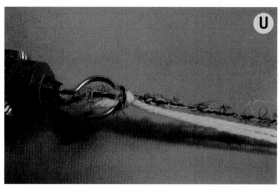

When you have decided on the required length, double it, then add on some extra for wastage at the ends, and add a bit more to allow for the fact that as the yarns are twisted they tend to reduce slightly in length. The tighter you twist, the more they will shrink, so it is a good idea to allow plenty of extra length.

Basically, cord is made by constructing twisted ply. You start with two or three (or more) long strands of yarn and anchor them at one end by tying the ends to a door handle or to another fixed object R (unless you have a very patient friend who will hold them for you!). Next, tie the other ends to a rod of some kind (such as a pencil) and, keeping the yarns taut, twist. Keep on twisting until you reach the stage where – if the yarns are allowed to go slack – they will form a tight coil S. When this happens you have probably twisted enough, so pull the yarns taut again and find the centre point of their length. Put your finger at the centre and allow the yarns to coil up from that point. You should then find that the entire length will coil up upon itself and you will end up with a twisted cord that is half (or slightly less than half) its original length T.

Obviously, if you want a very long piece of cord you will need a lot of space to do this. A large garden, hall or corridor will be required. Also, bear in mind that the longer the piece you are twisting, the longer it will take to twist sufficiently to form a coil – it takes far more twisting than you might think! To speed up the process, you can tie the non-anchored ends of the yarns to a cup-hook and put this in the jaws of an electric drill. Turn on the drill and you will find that the twisting is done at a much faster rate and will save you a lot of time U.

Glossary

Angelina fibres

Tiny, glittery threads of synthetic fibres, which melt and bond into a mesh when heat is applied.

Couching

A process whereby thick threads or yarns can be over-sewn with thinner thread. This can be done to decorate the yarn/thread and/or to sew the yarn onto a piece of fabric by over-sewing.

Dimensional fabric paint

A glutinous, pigmented substance that can be bought in tubs and squeezed onto fabric in small amounts for decorative purposes. It does not 'sink' into the fabric but sits on top and dries that way.

Embroidery foot

A special foot for the sewing machine that replaces the standard sewing foot when free-style embroidery is to be used. It is important that you get one that is designed especially for your particular make and model of machine.

Embroidery hoop

A circular frame (which can come in a variety of sizes) that stretches the fabric taut during sewing. It can be used in conjunction with a sewing machine and is particularly useful when sewing fine fabrics that lack stiffness.

Feed-dogs

These are the two rows of teeth under the sewing plate, which move the fabric along.

Free-style embroidery

By lowering or covering the feed-dogs on a sewing machine, the fabric can be moved in any direction by hand. This enables the sewer to fill in areas of fabric with blocks of random stitching.

Fusible interfacing

Adhesive-backed material that, when ironed onto fabric, will transfer the adhesive layer onto the fabric. Motifs can then be ironed on to the adhesive layer. Some forms of fusible interfacing have a piece of backing paper, which is peeled away after ironing.

Gutta

A type of fluid 'resist' used in silk painting for marking out sections of fabric.

Impact adhesive

A type of adhesive in which both surfaces are coated with a thin layer of the adhesive and left for a few minutes to go tacky. The surfaces are then pressed together to form a permanent bond.

Plain stitch

This is a standard straight stitch most commonly used for sewing two pieces of fabric together.

Pleat

A fold or tuck that is sewn into fabric.

Press-stud

A type of metal fastening consisting of two round metal halves which hold two pieces of fabric when snapped together.

Resist

This is a liquid substance that, when applied to fabric, resists the flow of dye. It is used for outlining designs onto fabric prior to painting them with dyes. Hot wax or gutta are both examples of resists.

Ruching

Creating folds in fabric.

Running stitch

This is a long stitch, usually sewn by hand along the edge of a piece of fabric, in order to gather it into folds when the thread is pulled from one end.

Satin-stitch

This is a zigzag machine-stitch where the stitches are very close together. It is a useful decorative stitch, particularly along edges.

Shirring

A method of ruching. This is a process whereby fabric is gathered into folds by means of a special elastic, called shirring elastic, in the bobbin.

Straight stitch

See 'Plain stitch'.

Tack

Baste. Large hand-stitches put in temporarily to hold two fabrics in place while machine stitching.

Top-stitch

A plain or straight stitch sewn onto the top surface of fabric, usually over a seam, to increase strength and add decoration.

Suppliers

UK

For beads:

Beads Direct
www.beadsdirect.co.uk
Tel: +44 (0)1509 852187
E-mail: service@beadsdirect.co.uk

Totallybeads
www.totallybeads.co.uk
Tel: +44 (0)1375 383531
E-mail: kitti@totallybeads.co.uk

For buckles:

Buckles Express
www.bucklesexpress.com
Tel: +44(0)1617 089541
E-mail: info@josephsegalltd.com

For buttons:

The Button Company
www.buttoncompany.co.uk
Tel: +44 (0)1243 775462
E-mail: info@buttoncompany.co.uk

For dyes:

Omega Dyes
www.omegadyes.co.uk
Tel: +44 (0)1453 823691
E-mail: omegadyes@abigailcrafts.co.uk

For handles:

Bags of Handles
www.bagsofhandles.co.uk
Tel: +44 (0)1394 279868
E-mail: webmaster@bagsofhandles.co.uk

For threads, yarns, ribbons and many other specialist products:

Nostalgia
www.nostalgiaribbon.com
Tel: +44 (0)1773 712240
E-mail: info@nostalgiaribbon.com

Stitch 'n' Craft
www.stitchncraft.co.uk
Tel: +44 (0)1747 852500
E-mail: enquiries@stitchncraft.co.uk

US

For fabrics:

Fabric Direct
www.fabricdirect.com
Tel: +1 (845) 679-2900
E-mail: info@fabricdirect.com

For handbag-making supplies:

UMX Universal Mercantile Exchange Inc.
www.umei.com
Tel: +1 (909) 839-0556
E-mail: sales@umei.com

For ribbons:

B.B. Crafts
www.bbcrafts.com
Tel: +1 (626) 968-8015
E-mail: support@bbcrafts.com

Bibliography

BANBURY, G. and DAWSON, P.
The Art of Painting on Silk
Search Press (1990)

BEAL, Margaret
Fusing Fabric
Batsford (2005)

BEANY, Jan
The Art of the Needle
Century (1988)

BRENNAN, Emma
Making Vintage Bags
GMC Publications (2005)

GREY, Maggie
Raising the Surface with Machine Embroidery
Batsford (2003)

LAWTHER, G.
*Inspirational Ideas for Embroidery on Clothes
    and Accessories*
Search Press (1993)

MEIN, Annemieke
The Art of Annemieke Mein, Wildlife Artist in Textiles
Search Press (2003)

WOLFF, Colette
The Art of Manipulating Fabric
Krause publications (1996)

About the author

Hilary Bowen was born in Dorchester, Dorset, in the south of England, and at the age of 18 moved to Hampshire, also southern England, where she completed a degree in Psychology. After graduating she taught in schools for a few years before completing a Masters degree and then teaching in Higher Education. She is currently a University lecturer.

Hilary has always been interested in a wide variety of Arts and Crafts and has experimented with several different media, including woodturning, photography and silver jewellery. Her interest in textile art led her to develop her skills in making evening bags, which became the subject of this book. She is quoted as saying:

"I love working with rich, colourful, tactile fabrics and trying out new techniques to create different effects."

Hilary has had two previous books published by GMC Publications: *Woodturning Jewellery* and *Decorative Techniques for Woodturners*.

Acknowledgements

With grateful thanks to Liz Randall for her help and advice.

Illustration: Patricia Briggs.

Additional Photography Credits

© GMC/Anthony Bailey:

p.4 right, all on pp. 6–7, bags on pp.8–9, p.13, p.17 far right top
and bottom, p.19, p.25, p.29 bottom, p.31, p.35, p.41, pp.46–47,
p.51, p.57, p.63, p.69, p.75, p.81, pp.86–87, p.91

Courtesy of morguefile.com:

p.4 left 'markmiller', p.5 'markmiller', p.8 top 'bowlingranny',
centre 'chamomile', bottom left 'phaewilk', p.9 top 'clarita',
p.12 top 'clarita', centre 'markmiller', bottom 'click',
background 'lensfushion', p.18 top 'giggs', centre 'mconnors',
bottom 'mindweb ', background 'solrac-gi-2nd', p.24 all 'loneangel',
p.30 top 'kabir', bottom 'pindiyath100', background 'rollingroscoe',
p.34 top 'phaewilk', centre 'idahoeditor', bottom 'beat0092',
p.40 top 'keithrichardson', centre 'ladycaroler', p.50 top 'chamomile',
centre 'bowlingranny', bottom 'phaewilk', p.56 top' mconnors',
bottom 'idahoeditor', background 'southernfried', p.62 top 'luisrock62',
bottom 'bowlingranny', p.68 top 'clarita', bottom 'luisrock62',
p.74 bottom 'clarita', background 'bowlingranny', p.80 top 'mensatic',
p.90 top 'dave', centre 'clarita', background 'rosevita'

All other photographs not already credited on imprint page:

p.34 background © Dominique Page,
p.80 centre and background © Corbis

Index

GMC Publications
Castle Place, 166 High Street, Lewes
East Sussex, BN7 1XU
United Kingdom

Tel: 01273 488005
Fax: 01273 402866
E-mail: pubs@thegmcgroup.com
Website: www.gmcbooks.com

Contact us for a complete catalogue, or visit our website.
Orders by credit card are accepted.